INNER COMPASS
MOM

DANIELLE KLOBERDANZ

Danielle Kloberdanz

INNER COMPASS
MOM

DANIELLE KLOBERDANZ

Build. Buzz. Launch.
Media & Publishing
Dallas, TX

First published by Danielle Kloberdanz, 2021

Published by BBL Publishing, an imprint of
Build.Buzz.Launch. Media & Publishing, Dallas TX, 75218
www.buildbuzzlaunch.com

BBL
PUBLISHING

First Edition 2021

21 22 23 24 25 / 10 9 8 7 6 5 4 3 2 1
ISBN 978-1-7352966-0-9
Library of Congress Control Number: 2021901719

Creative Direction: Kaspar deLine – deLine & Co.
Cover Photograph: Sam Edwards I iStock Photo

Manufactured in the United States of America

Manufactured in the United States of America

For print copies, author interviews contact:
info@buildbuzzlaunch.com

Contents

Preface

The journey of motherhood is an incredible dive into the unknown. Even the best parenting advice from books or other sources cannot prepare us for all that lies ahead with our families. So, becoming a mom means taking a leap of faith and learning as we go. And now, as we are dealing with a global pandemic and economic crisis, we are asked once again to find that same courage and faith to help us navigate unfamiliar territories.

There is no question about how challenging, depressing, or even devastating this time for many of us is. However, this *Great Pause*, as some refer to this historic moment in time, is possibly our greatest opportunity for getting off the treadmill of our busy lives. No longer speeding through it, we have a chance to reflect and decide if we want to get back on that same treadmill one day, or if we want to make some lasting changes in the way we manage our families and other areas of our lives.

This is exactly what *Inner Compass Mom* is all about: it is a guide to help you reflect on your life and the various roles you play; a roadmap to help you courageously and honestly ask yourself what you'd love to expand or pursue in your life and what you'd wish to reduce or eliminate. *Inner Compass Mom* will help you gently navigate the process of finding your deepest truths so you can create a life that is more closely aligned with your soul's longing, with the authentic you.

My hope is that this book will show you how to tune into your inner compass to help reveal your *True North*: the direction in which your soul wants to journey. When you look the other way, when you ignore your soul's deepest desires, unhappiness and other negative emotions arise. But when you find the courage to move beyond your fears and false beliefs of who you think you are or should be, you uncover your *true self*. When you follow your *True North*, you will experience more inner peace and a deeper sense of purpose, no matter what challenges arise.

So here's to all you moms out there. Wherever you are in the world, whichever phase of life you are in, and whichever challenge you may be faced with, I encourage you to connect to your inner compass and find your peace and purpose.

– Danielle Kloberdanz

Introduction

I had the perfect life: a great partnership with my husband, four healthy kids, financial prosperity, and a beautiful house in a Southern California town with parks and pools and high performing schools. I was living the dream. I should have been full of life, vibrant with possibilities and plans. Instead, I felt exhausted and drained. I yearned for more meaning beyond my role as a stay-at-home parent. I was stuck in disappointment and disillusionment.

My longing for more meaning led me into a life-changing spiritual awakening from which I gained a profound new understanding of motherhood. For several days, I was in a higher state of consciousness which gave me fresh perspectives on what it means to be human at this time in history. This transformation released me from a lifetime of believing that I wasn't good enough. I understood how this false belief, and many others that I held, dictated the way I was living my life and how I parented. As a result of this spiritual awakening, I have a renewed awareness in my parenting and even greater passion for what I want to pursue in my life.

Life today seems more complex than ever before, with endless options and opportunities. This can be exciting, but it can also leave us feeling overwhelmed and confused. Outside forces may disconnect us from our inner compass — the intuitive instinct that shows us which direction to go next. In our fast-paced world, it's easy to lose ourselves and get caught up in some race for outward victories and so-called successes that only temporarily fulfill us. In the long run, they leave us wondering about our investments of time, money, and effort.

Our inner compass is always with us. It's our soul. It never fails to point to our True North, guiding us toward becoming the highest expression of ourselves, beyond our fears and false beliefs of who we think we are or who we should be. Following our inner compass takes courage, but beyond our deepest fears lies a world of wisdom to help us conquer them, clearing a new path of possibilities.

If you are a seeker of meaning and purpose, yearning to know yourself deeply, or want to rediscover long lost dreams or find a better sense of direction in your life, perhaps beyond your role as a mother, this book will help you. The tools I discuss, along with my own experiences, will show you how to tune in to your inner compass so it can guide you on your journey of uncovering your truths and bringing forth the very best expression of your most brilliant self.

PART ONE
GETTING STUCK

How I Got Stuck in Life

" 'What is the world's greatest lie?' the boy asked, completely surprised.
'It is this: that at a certain point in our lives, we lose control
of what is happening to us, and our lives become controlled by fate.
That is the world's greatest lie.' "

— Paulo Coelho, The Alchemist

I t's easy to become trapped in the belief that our lives are controlled by fate and that there is not much we can do about it. At one time or another most of us may feel stuck in a career or relationship, victimized by destiny or karma. Random events seem to happen beyond our control. They can affect us deeply and leave us with mixed emotions such as frustration, anger, and fear. Our destiny appears to be mysteriously unfolding without us having much say in it. This is the lie that I was stuck in.

In 2013 I was a 41-year-old, stay-at-home mom of four children ranging in age from three to eleven. I was in a great marriage, had healthy kids, and lived in a wonderful neighborhood with great schools, yet I was not happy and felt something was missing. Raising kids was much harder than I'd expected and not as satisfying as I had hoped. Life felt like it was closing in on me, leaving me fewer options instead of fulfilling the grand dreams and possibilities of my youth. Instead of feeling grateful for all the gifts in my life, I felt stifled — suffocated.

I was born and raised in The Netherlands, also called Holland. For as long as I can remember, I longed to be a stay-at-home mom. I didn't care much

"I wanted a big family with lots of kids running around the house spreading their joy and liveliness."

about having a career. I wanted a big family with lots of kids running around the house spreading their joy and liveliness. My family of origin consisted of my parents and my two older sisters. We girls were all a couple of years apart. I had several aunts, uncles, and cousins, but they lived far away. After my parents divorced when I was ten, those connections grew strained and we rarely saw our relatives. As a result, I didn't grow up with a large extended family that I longed for.

Several of our friends and neighbors had big families though, including the family who lived across the street from us. They had four — no, "Oops, we're having another one!" — five kids. Both parents came from large families so there were lots of extended family members around, too. I was their babysitter and they always made me feel like I was part of the family. I loved being invited to birthday parties, graduations, and other celebrations. During those events, their home was filled with laughter and animated conversations. Theirs was the kind of home life I yearned to have when I grew up.

Fast forward a few years later to my sister's wedding in Northern California. This was an exciting event, not only because my sister was getting married (to an American man!), but also because I had never been to the U.S. I was twenty-five and thrilled to travel to this amazing destination. After being a tourist for a couple of weeks, the wedding day finally arrived. And that's when it happened for me. I met the love of my life at my sister's wedding.

The wedding was a three-day event, and many of us helped set up and decorate the wedding venue, including Jim, who had been the groom's college roommate. The first things I noticed about Jim were his vibrant blue eyes and the warm tone in his voice. During breaks, Jim threw a football with some of the other guys. I couldn't help but notice his strong arms in his tight, white t-shirt.

He was tall with broad shoulders, wavy brown hair, and kind eyes. Every now and then I caught him looking my way and beamed back a shy smile.

Jim and I got to know each other better at the wedding reception. Even though I was a bit shy and not that confident in my English skills, he had a way about him that made me feel comfortable talking to him. He lived in Southern California, held a job as an accountant, and played guitar and sang at coffee houses in his free time. After the reception ended, I was invited to join him and some of his friends in an empty dining room of the hotel where he played guitar for us. I was captivated by his talent and enjoyed listening to him for about an hour until we got kicked out by the concierge. A guest had complained about the noise. We called it a night and went our separate ways to our hotel rooms. I was mortified the next morning when I discovered that my dad was the guest who had complained about the music.

After breakfast the next day, Jim hugged me goodbye and suggested we stay in touch. I was relieved he seemed interested in me, and I heartily agreed, even though I was living in Holland at the time. He offered to mail me a copy of the demo tape he'd made when he'd attempted to launch his music career. I gladly accepted. A couple of weeks later I was thrilled to receive Jim's tape. I loved hearing his voice again. Many nights I fell asleep listening to his songs, which were mostly covers but included a couple of originals. His gift intrigued me and made me want to get to know this great guy even more.

Jim visited me in Holland a couple of months after we met, and we officially started dating. Our whirlwind romance was a magical time and played out all over Europe, including in Barcelona, Brugge, and Prague, as well as Southern California. It was wonderful getting to know each other better over romantic dinners and frequent leisurely strolls through the streets of those enchanting cities. Between visits we wrote letters back and forth and talked on the phone. We were madly in love and, during our visit to Prague, he popped the question. We couldn't wait to share the exciting news with everyone! A few weeks later, we married in Holland in the beautiful 500 year-old City Hall of Alkmaar, the town in which I was born. After just nine months of dating and many letters, phone calls, faxes, and emails, we were married. I immigrated to the U.S. a couple of months later in 1998, shortly after my 26th birthday.

"I questioned my fitness as a mother. I could barely manage caring for two children."

Jim and I decided to postpone having children for a couple of years until he finished his MBA. While he went to graduate school, I held a couple of office jobs and later worked with autistic children in a school. I had gone to college and studied developmental psychology, but I'd never held a job in my field of study. More than any career, I wanted to be a full-time mom. I enjoyed working with the autistic children, but it wasn't a deep passion for me so much as a way to spend my time until I had a family of my own.

Our first child arrived in 2002 when I was 30. For years I had looked forward to walking around with a big pregnant belly, proudly announcing to the world the imminent arrival of our bundle of joy. However, disappointment and worry flooded me when I was put on bedrest halfway through my pregnancy. I spent weeks in bed or on the couch ruminating over my fears of further complications. Jim had just turned in his last paper to complete his MBA. We'd planned to spend our final months of freedom together taking some short trips before the baby was born, now that Jim was no longer spending extra time on homework in addition to working a full-time job. I felt bad about disappointing him. Bedrest meant no traveling, no dinners out, no sunsets on the beach. We had no choice but to accept the situation, so we made the best of it.

All went well and a few months later, we had our baby girl. We were over the moon. As we adjusted to the sleepless nights, the diaper changing, nursing around-the-clock, and the many other challenges new parents face in the first year, I longed for another child. I got pregnant right away and after another complicated pregnancy, including three months of bedrest, I gave birth to another girl in 2004.

Our daughters were nineteen months apart, which proved to be quite a challenge. Both kids needed lots of attention. I was pulled back and forth between a crying baby who needed to nurse or have a diaper changed, and an almost two-year-old who didn't understand she had to wait her turn to receive my attention. Many times, my frustration with this situation made me question my fitness as a mother. I had no choice but to keep going, hoping things would get easier over time. We got some extra help from family and Jim took time off from work when he could. During this time, Jim's career picked up. He worked about sixty hours a week and travelled a lot, so I felt like a single parent. I couldn't imagine having more children. I was overwhelmed and disappointed. My dream of a large family didn't seem realistic. I could barely manage caring for two children.

After a couple of years, when it became easier to manage the girls, I started dreaming of having another child. I couldn't see how it would work with our current situation though. On top of Jim's busy career, Jim was now in his mid-forties and I was in my mid-thirties. Even though we had always envisioned having three or four children, we had entered age groups with increased risks of having children with health challenges.

In 2006, when our youngest was about two years old, I had a routine health check. My bloodwork showed an extremely low platelet count. I was sent to a hematologist who told me the low platelet count indicated a possible immune disorder, such as leukemia, or MS. I was shocked. I never thought something like this would happen to me. I felt healthy, after all. My naturopathic doctor suggested I stop taking my birth control, which could have caused the drop in my platelet count. I took her advice, and over the next several months my bloodwork improved.

One day, I received the news I had deeply been hoping for: a clean bill of health. After the appointment, I sat in my car as tears filled my eyes and gratitude filled my heart. I had gotten a second chance at living a healthy life. What did I want to do with it?

I knew exactly what I wanted: more children. I wanted to stop living in fear and embrace life. Yes, we were getting older, increasing our risk of having babies with health challenges, and my pregnancies were difficult, but I had gotten through them. I wasn't a perfect mom, but I had connected to enough other moms to know I wasn't the only one feeling uncertain about parenting. I didn't want to be finished having babies. I realized there are no guarantees in life, so I might as well take a chance and fulfill my dream of having a big family.

Soon we went through some big changes, including a move from Orange County to San Diego and a new, more manageable job for Jim. It was 2008, and I was 36. We lived closer to family; and Jim had a short commute to his job and could spend more time with me and the children. Life was more balanced. It felt as though we had started a new chapter. We appreciated our new family-friendly neighborhood with parks and pools for us to enjoy. Life was more relaxed and seemed to leave some space for another child. After a few months of settling in, we tried to get pregnant. Sure enough, I conceived right away and, midway through the pregnancy, I was put on bedrest once again, just like the other times. We made it through, and, four weeks earlier than planned, we welcomed our third girl into our growing family. We were delighted with another healthy baby girl.

Having a third child almost seemed easier in a lot of ways. Our two older girls were quite independent at four and almost six, and I was a more seasoned mom. It was a joy spending time with our sweet, easygoing baby. Her older sisters adored her and were my little helpers. Sibling rivalry didn't seem to be an issue.

A year later, we tried for a fourth baby so that each child would have a playmate close in age. Unfortunately, I miscarried twice and went through a trying time of reflection and doubt. *Why was this happening to me?* I had been convinced we'd have four children, because that felt so right to me. Now, I felt so lost. I wondered if we were meant to have a fourth. And, because I'd always gotten pregnant easily, I was scared to try again. I wondered how many times I'd be willing to get pregnant and miscarry again before I'd give up my dream of having a fourth child.

After a few months of uncertainty, I was guided by a powerful dream that convinced me I was meant to have another baby and that we shouldn't wait any longer. As soon as I woke up, I felt transformed. I basked in gratitude for the guidance I had received. I became pregnant quickly, and after yet another challenging pregnancy, we welcomed our son in 2010.

"My entire identity was wrapped up in being a mother, and I was falling far short of my expectations of myself."

With the fourth child, our family felt complete. I was 38, had two school-age children, a toddler, and a newborn. I'd gotten everything I wanted: a loving husband who I could always count on and who provided so well for us that I didn't have to work, a houseful of healthy children, and a gorgeous home. I was exhausted, but I figured over time it would get easier, just like it had when our first two were out of the baby and toddler phases. I did my best to juggle various schedules for school, sports, playdates, birthday parties, etc., while trying to maintain my relationship with my husband. I tried to soak up the many precious moments of sweet smiles and giggles, of first steps and first words, of heartwarming Mother's Day cards with squiggle drawings and misspelled words, while attempting to ignore the chaos and challenges of the day.

Over time, some things did get easier, but other things got harder. The daily challenges of raising four completely different personalities and the children's after-school activities added a perpetual stress that put me on edge. I tried to push my growing disappointment away and hang in there, consoling myself with the thought that I'd have my freedom back when our youngest went to college. But that meant I was looking at fifteen more years of hanging in there! It seemed like an eternity. Some days I couldn't imagine how I would ever get through it.

Deep down, I was embarrassed to admit that I felt disappointed with my wonderful life. I'd wanted all of my children with all of my heart, but on tough days I felt like a loser. I was supposed to be a great mom who could do it all — the cooking, the cleaning, the errands, the baths — with endless patience. My entire identity was wrapped up in being a mother, and I was falling far short of my expectations of myself. Since I didn't have a successful career to be

" I had to figure out how to glean
more fulfillment and happiness
from the life I was already living, not
create distractions from it."

proud of outside of motherhood, I was overwhelmed with discouragement and could not shake the feeling that I wasn't succeeding at anything.

As the years went on, I could no longer convince myself that my life was good in so many ways and that I shouldn't complain. I longed for room to breathe. I sensed I needed to expand my horizon beyond motherhood. Volunteering at our elementary school made me feel useful and appreciated. I also loved connecting with other moms. It was a nice change of pace, but I wanted something else. I sensed getting a job outside of the home would be an escape, but it wouldn't truly satisfy me. I couldn't help but think there was a deeper, more fulfilling purpose waiting for me; I just had no idea what it was. I sensed that I had to figure out how to glean more fulfillment and happiness from the life I was already living, not create distractions from it. There had to be more to my life than the daily grind of childcare and household duties. I longed for moments of solitude to reflect on how I was going to make a change. Although I didn't know what the change would look like, I figured taking some quiet time for myself was a good place to start. Solitude would create the space I desperately needed to explore what I wanted to pursue next. My desperation had grown strong enough to convince me to claim this space for myself.

In the next chapters, I share with you how I shifted from feeling stuck to creating the freedom that allowed me to sense my next steps towards more fulfillment and meaning. I explain and illustrate through my own experiences how to use the various tools that helped me create this shift while I uncovered my authentic self along the way. These tools worked for me, and they can do the same for you.

PART ONE
GETTING STUCK
SUMMARY POINTS

- You feel stuck when you think that you have no control over your life.

- Awareness of what is within your control opens the way to new possibilities.

- High expectations can set you up for disappointment.

- Acknowledgment of feeling unfulfilled is necessary to make change possible.

- Negative emotions such as overwhelm, sadness, or anger are signals from your inner compass to explore a different path.

- Give yourself permission to explore what is possible for you.

PART TWO
FOLLOWING YOUR INNER COMPASS

Finding Your Center

*"The path of peace appears to be a fight, but it isn't. It's the art of
filling up what's missing and emptying out what is superfluous."*

— *Paulo Coelho, Aleph*

Finding your way back to your center means finding a calmer place
within you. Paulo Coelho describes it beautifully in the quote
above. Stress and busyness can easily distract you, pulling you away
from what matters most, including your heart's desires and dreams.
Tools such as solitude, journaling, and meditation can help you connect to
your true purpose and goals.

SOLITUDE

Solitude grants access to deeper thinking, reflecting, and analyzing. It's
important to create moments of alone time on a regular basis so that
you can connect with deeper layers of yourself. To follow a path of
more fulfillment, joy, and purpose, you first need to explore what might
create those feelings inside you. Solitude allows you to tune into your
intuition — your inner compass. When you permit yourself to explore
your soul's longings and act upon this inspiration, over time you create
inner balance, peace, and fulfillment. Solitude is necessary on the path
of conscious awakening for discovering who you truly are and what you

Solitude is a state of being alone that you
deliberately choose because you want to
connect more deeply with yourself.

most want to do with your life. It brings you closer to your authentic
purpose. Through solitude I found many answers to the questions I had
about my life's meaning and purpose. I was able to sense what I truly
wanted and needed, not through being busier and working harder but
rather through slowing down.

During the years that I still had a toddler at home, I had increasingly
more time to myself. Our boy entertained himself quite nicely, allowing
me to do my chores peacefully much of the time. In those quiet moments,
I realized how much I craved solitude. I longed to read inspiring books
again. I hadn't read a book in years, but now I was ready for information on
spirituality and psychology. I wanted to know if there was a deeper meaning
to my life beyond raising children, and if so, what it was. As a teenager and
young adult, I had been fascinated by the mystical aspects of life, but the
perpetual tasks of raising my children had pushed that interest to some
far corner of my awareness. I hoped that reading inspiring books, such as
Autobiography of a Yogi by Paramahansa Yogananda or Shakti Gawain's
Creative Visualization which I read in my younger years, would reconnect
me to that passion again.

I started with *The Alchemist* by Paulo Coelho. I came upon the book quite
by chance, or perhaps divine intervention, as I was shopping at Costco. I
had never heard of the book or the author, but it caught my eye. It remains
one of the most inspirational books I have read. *The Alchemist* inspired
me so much that I wrote the many insights it gave me down in a journal. I
continued doing this with other books too and started journaling on how

those insights were connected to my experiences. Bit by bit, I started to breathe and to feel energized again.

Solitude doesn't mean loneliness, which is more a sad feeling about being alone. You can feel lonely even while you're surrounded by others if you don't feel connected to them. Solitude is a state of being alone that you deliberately choose because you want to connect more deeply with yourself. Solitude allows you to create space in which to explore what you want to let go of, and what you want to draw into your life. This personal space offers an opportunity to reflect on yourself and your life. You can delve into your inner world of thoughts and feelings and reflect on your desires, fears, and beliefs.

STRESS

Sometimes it's hard to be by yourself, especially when you're not yet accustomed to solitude. It was easy for me to be alone while reading interesting books because they inspired me and I was learning something. However, it was a different story when it came to being in solitude without doing anything. In those moments I was restless and uncomfortable. Not only did I have to deal with my own judgemental mind about how I was wasting my time as I went through a mental to-do list, I was also detoxing from the constant stress of my hectic lifestyle.

Many of us are habitually on-the-go much of the time. It's as though we don't know how to have downtime anymore, don't know how to just be without doing anything, or without entertainment from our phones or devices. We often use our level of busyness, our jam-packed schedule, as a measurement of success or even self-worth. It seems as if we have fewer moments of uninterrupted solitude today than we did ten or fifteen years ago.

Stress hormones are addictive. According to Dr. Heidi Hanna of The American Institute of Stress, "Stress may even be as addictive as drugs. In addition to the hormones adrenaline and noradrenaline, stress also releases dopamine, a 'feel good' chemical. Dopamine encourages repeat behaviors by activating the reward center in our brain and may be at the heart of many addictive behaviors and substance abuse issues."

It takes practice to rest in a state of simply being, but there are many advantages to the deep relaxation that this state can bring us. Dr. Hanna reminds us, "It's important that we recognize the significance of what a stress imbalance does to our system, physically, emotionally, mentally, and spiritually."

Over time I have learned to let go of guilt for taking time for myself. I now know the value of recharging and balancing myself. I can better handle anything that comes my way when I'm centered and fully present in my life.

At one particularly difficult period in my life, one thing after another seemed to come crashing down on me. On top of the usual demands of keeping a family of six going with multiple schedules, multiple schools, and various individual demands, extra challenges had crossed my path with some of my kids, along with other family struggles. This situation left me feeling overwhelmed and filled me with worry and heaviness. I felt I'd reached the limit of what I could handle. Exhaustion was a heavy blanket weighing me down. I could see it in the dark circles under my eyes. I had been on a bad streak of drinking extra coffee to deal with my exhaustion due to a lack of sleep. On top of that I consumed more sweets, which made me feel worse, and I hadn't taken a yoga class in weeks. I had to turn things around and find a healthy way to decompress.

So one Monday morning I made some herbal tea instead of a second cup of coffee and went to one of our beautiful neighborhood parks. It was amazingly quiet and peaceful on this sunny autumn day. A tree at the edge of the park caught my eye. It was hidden from view from the street, overlooking a canyon. I put my phone on do-not-disturb mode and laid down in the grass underneath the tree.

As I looked up at the green canopy overhead, I observed the leaves and branches swaying in the breeze, exposing snippets of the blue sky with their movement. I knew from past experience that my ruminations weren't going to solve anything, and that the way out of my heaviness was by letting go of my worry-filled thoughts. I tried to become one with the movement of the tree and mentally repeated the mantra, "Let go," as I exhaled. After a while,

"Journaling, meditating, spending time
in nature, and creating artwork are other
ways to connect with your inner compass."

I noticed my body relaxing, as though the breeze had carried away some of my worries, leaving me with a sense of serenity. Later I took a yoga class, and that night I went to bed early and had the best night's sleep I'd had in years.

The next morning, I felt rejuvenated and, once again, had a more optimistic outlook on life, even though nothing had changed about my circumstances. I was very grateful for this shift and for listening to what I'd sensed I needed. It was worth it to take that time to myself and slow down.

Being connected to how you feel, acknowledging what you need, and acting upon it can help you stay centered and better handle life's challenges without burning out or breaking down. If you want to connect with yourself at a deeper level and move closer to discovering what is purposeful to you, you'll have to get comfortable with quieting your mind and calming your body. It takes time and practice to get beyond the layers of thinking, worrying, and feelings of anger and frustration to reach a heightened state of awareness and get in touch with your deeper truths.

Centering practices can be helpful for moving beyond your worries, ruminations, frustrations, and anger, or anything else that overwhelms you. I remember feeling very sorry for myself one morning. But, no matter how much I believed my self-pity was justified, it didn't make me feel any better. Once I realized how stuck I was in this emotional state, I thought about the different ways I'd learned to create a positive shift in my thinking and feeling. It seemed a good time to apply them. I remembered a line from the prayer of St. Francis: "It is in giving that we receive." I realized that many people are in worse situations than me, or at least have serious problems too, and that

"Journaling is a great tool on the path towards more fulfillment."

praying for others can have a healing effect on the person praying as well as on those being prayed for. I decided to try it.

I thought of several people I knew who had challenges in their lives and I started sending them positive thoughts. It was amazing how quickly my energy shifted from feeling deeply hurt, which was an ache in my gut, to the sensation of warmth flowing from the top of my head through my entire body. I instantly felt relieved and was able to let go of my self-pity. As I prayed, it released what was blocked inside of me. What I received was a more peaceful, uplifted state of being.

Prayer is one of the many tools you can use to center yourself. Journaling, meditating, spending time in nature, and creating artwork are other ways to connect with your inner compass. Using these tools, you can tune into a version of yourself that is less rigid, more fluid. These activities can slow down your busy, often judgemental mind.

Centering is like the slowing down of a churning river into an easy flowing stream. When your mind enters a more tranquil state you can sense a deep-seated state of consciousness that offers you glimpses of who you truly are. This awareness, beyond the logical mind with all its censorship, fills you with renewed inspiration and passion, and guides you towards more clarity about how to move forward in life.

JOURNALING

Journaling helps process emotions and aids in clarifying your thoughts by forcing you to put words to them. This can help you let them go so they are no longer front-and-center of your attention. You can leave your worries and frustrations on the paper, making it easier to connect to your inner compass.

Writing to tap into a stream of consciousness can help you access a more creative, flowing state of mind. In *The Artist's Way*, Julia Cameron suggests writing morning pages each day. You write three full pages of whatever comes to mind to help you move beyond your critical mind into your creativity. This process unblocks fears and judgements so you can reach the quiet center within yourself and connect with your inner compass.

I often use writing to help me unblock and get into a state of relaxation and flow. As my pencil flows over the paper in a slow and steady pace, I start to relax. I continue writing slowly, focusing on the letters that form and how the pencil feels in my hand, until I feel a shift. I don't focus much on the content of my writing at first, but rather on the motion of putting words on the page. I simply start the process and trust that ideas will spring up as I continue. I'm amazed every time at how much clearer my thoughts are and how much I enjoy being in this deeply relaxed and inspired state. Once I have flow, I move to my computer and start typing.

I naturally fell into journaling. I started with writing down the insights I gleaned in books I was reading. I reflected on the insights and made connections to my own experiences. Over time, I noticed I thoroughly enjoyed the process of writing. There was something energizing about introspection, about examining ideas, philosophies, and experiences while writing about them. I've discovered that the more I write without judgement, the more I experience a state of flow. This relaxes me and opens up a portal of new ideas, inspiration, and an ability to see connections between ideas and experiences more clearly, sometimes creating astonishing moments of synchronicity.

I remember one of those moments. It was evening, and after a busy day with the kids, I needed some down time. I went to bed early to read for a while. As I went through my bedtime routine, I recalled an event from many years ago that had impacted me significantly. I went way down memory lane, recalling many details from an encounter with a coyote during a walk in a local canyon.

At that point in my life, 17 years earlier, I had felt lost, with no clear sense of direction. I was 27 and had only lived in the U.S. for one year. I wasn't happy with my job then, but Jim and I weren't ready to have kids yet. I thought that a walk in the canyon might do me some good and ease my melancholy. I followed a different path than usual. The trail sloped down into a small, grassy clearing bordered by a narrow creek in the distance, and heavy shrubs and trees on my left and right.

As I made my way down, I became a bit anxious. A fly wouldn't leave me alone. Then some dry brush scratched my leg. I decided to go back up the trail. When I reached the top, I took one more look at the beautiful scenery. I soaked up the serenity of the moment, absorbing the balmy air and the buzzing sounds of nature. Then I heard a noise below me. A deer jumped out, raced across the valley, and disappeared into the trees. A coyote followed. To my surprise, it stopped in the middle of the clearing and looked around. When our eyes met, I froze, fearing it would attack me. With all my senses fully awakened, I decided to run for it. My heart raced as I turned and sped as fast as I could back to safety. My earlier feelings of dullness were gone, replaced with a deep sense of gratitude for the amazing experience that had made me feel more alive than I'd felt in a long time.

As I recalled the details of this event, 17 years later, I decided to write down all that I remembered. I reached for a notebook in my nightstand drawer and noticed my old dream diaries from my teenage and college years. During those years I'd had many vivid dreams, and instead of keeping a journal I'd kept dream diaries. I decided to look at them after I wrote down what I remembered.

As I wrote the story of meeting the coyote I relaxed and moved into flow, a wonderful, calm, and peaceful state of being. After I finished writing I was excited to go back in time by reading some of my old diaries. I randomly opened one. To my amazement, I opened to the page on which I had written the same story about the coyote encounter 17 years ago. It was as though I had energetically connected to it and opened to the page with that story.

Synchronicity often results from tapping into this kind of flow state. Gregg Levoy from PsychologyToday.com explains what synchronicity is:

Synchronicities are events connected to one another not

by strict cause-and-effect, but by what in classical times were known as *sympathies*, by the belief that an acausal relationship exists between events on the inside and the outside of ourselves, a crosstalk between mind and matter —which is governed by a certain species of attraction.

He reminds us that "Jung called synchronicity *meaningful coincidence*." Levoy continues:

A synchronicity is a coincidence that has an analog in the psyche, and depending on how you understand it, it can inform you, primarily through intuition and emotion, how near or far you are from what Carlos Castaneda calls *the path with heart*. Among shamanic cultures, says anthropologist Michael Harner in *The Way of the Shaman*, synchronicities are considered "a kind of homing beacon analogous to a radio directional signal indicating that the right procedures and methods are being employed."

My moment of synchronicity about the coyote encounter validated to me that I had indeed connected to a deeper, more intuitive part of myself. This energized me and filled me with a renewed sense of awe for the mysteries of life.

If you don't have a regular practice of journaling but would like to try it, there are a few things to keep in mind. First, make sure you keep your journal completely private. This eliminates one layer of fear of judgement.

Second, you'll have to learn to handle your inner critic. This gets easier over time as you grow more accustomed to writing about your inner world. Try stream-of-consciousness writing, like Julia Cameron suggests with her morning pages exercise: "The morning pages are the primary tool of creative recovery. As blocked artists, we tend to criticize ourselves mercilessly. Even if we look like functioning artists to the world, we feel we never do enough and what we do isn't right."

Even though Cameron writes about artists, her ideas apply to all of us who are feeling blocked or stuck in some area of our lives. She explains

"You can leave your worries and frustrations on the paper, making it easier to connect to your inner compass."

that we have an inner critic that she calls The Censor. Writing morning pages, putting down anything that comes to mind, especially all the negative thoughts we have about ourselves and our abilities, will help us get these out of our mind. Cameron suggests the following rule: "Always remember that your Censor's negative opinions are not the truth." Journaling might be uncomfortable at first, but it gets easier over time. The more honest you can be with yourself, the better you'll get to know yourself and identify what you truly want and desire.

Third, practice. The more often you write, the easier it gets.

Fourth, when you feel like abandoning your journaling practice, remind yourself why you started doing it in the first place: to help you create a positive shift in your life. Reminding yourself can help you get back into it.

Journaling can be extremely helpful for creating more fulfillment in your life. Not only is journaling a great way to center yourself through the process of letting go of what preoccupies you, it can also clear mental confusion or a tendency toward distracting yourself with busyness. Journaling can help you understand yourself better so that over time, you have a deeper understanding about what truly brings you happiness and joy.

Keeping a journal can also help you keep track of your progress. During times in which you feel stagnant, you can look back and see that you've moved forward in some areas. You might have better insights into what you want and don't want. You might be better at using journaling as a centering tool, letting go of whatever preoccupies you. You might notice the hesitation in your writing when you first started, and how you are now able to write with abandon. Journaling is a great tool on the path towards more fulfillment. Once you know what you want, you can start using other tools to help you achieve your goals.

MEDITATION AND PRAYER

While journaling helps you process your emotions and clarify your thoughts, meditation allows you to practice letting go of your thinking and feeling self altogether and achieve a mentally clear and emotionally calm state. Spiritual guru Deepak Chopra says, "Meditation provides experiences that the mind can achieve no other way, such as inner silence and expanded awareness."

Your identity is shaped over the course of your lifetime. How you see yourself is largely influenced by values you've internalized from your parents and your culture, and by how your loved ones and peers see you. Ideas and values coming from outside of you, internalized by your ego, can throw off the signals originating from your inner compass, often leaving you confused as to what is truly coming from within.

Your inner compass always points to your True North. Your soul knows your deeper purpose and what would be joyful and meaningful to you, but when you've been exposed to ideas from your culture and environment long enough, it becomes harder to sense where your True North is pointing and which path or beliefs resonate most authentically with you. This is why stilling the mind with meditation practices is so important. Quieting your thoughts allows for a deeper, more authentic truth to arise. The path of spiritual awakening involves uncovering the values and ideas that are authentic to you, regardless of what others think. Sometimes it takes "unlearning" much of what you've learned through social conditioning by questioning the many beliefs you've held so that more authentic perspectives can arise within you.

You are not your thoughts. In meditation, you increase the gaps between thoughts so a different awareness can come through. When you learn to let go of your thoughts by redirecting your focus onto your breath, a guided meditation, or a mantra, you experience a different kind of knowing. This awareness taps into who you truly are, at the level of your soul, beyond the mental identity of who you think you are, i.e., your ego.

In The *Power of Now* Eckhart Tolle says:

> So the single most vital step on your journey toward
> enlightenment is this: learn to disidentify from your mind.
> Every time you create a gap in the stream of mind, the
> light of your consciousness grows stronger. One day you
> may catch yourself smiling at the voice in your head,
> as you would smile at the antics of a child. This means that
> you no longer take the content of your mind all that
> seriously, as your sense of self does not depend on it.

Tolle's wisdom about witnessing our thoughts helped me tremendously with disidentifying myself from my mind. I remember how amazed I was when I read this and then asked myself, *Who is the witness?* I immediately sensed the separation between me (the witness) and my thoughts. When we experience this separation, it becomes easier to shift our focus away from our thoughts and become the objective witness.

In observing your thoughts without engaging with them through judgements or opinions coupled with emotional reactions, you experience simply being. You connect to your true essence. There is still consciousness, but it's different from thinking: it's awareness. Unlike thinking, which can be obsessive and ruminative, awareness is a calm, deep knowing. It's observing without judgement. Judgement involves ego and identification with your mind, with who you think you are. You are far more than what your conditioned mind believes. When you sink deeper into this state of being, of observing, you step out of ordinary time and space reality and perceive a bigger picture of life, which offers you new insights and wisdom. A deep sense of peace and wellbeing is often the result.

Many of us have had glimpses of an expanded state of awareness. It can happen when we're caught by surprise by stunning natural scenery that takes our breath away, like a sunset lighting the sky on fire. Or when the endless black sky filled with radiant stars gives us a taste of infinity. In these moments, our mind stops thinking and we are in awe. Even if it's just for a split second,

"You are far more than what your conditioned mind believes."

a new awareness floods us. It can be felt as a sense of the expansiveness of the universe, or an awareness of timelessness, or feeling connected to something greater than ourselves.

In order to experience this awareness, you must minimize distractions from outside sources and from your busy mind. Nowadays many of us live with elevated stress levels, either due to worries about various areas in our lives (money, health, career, relationships), an overly busy schedule, or spending too much time on electronic devices. Whenever you prepare to meditate, reduce sensory stimulation to your nervous system, especially noise and visual stimuli such as from computers, phones, tablets, and TVs. If you experience lots of resistance to meditation or have tried it before and feel it simply doesn't work for you, it can help to reflect on your daily activities. Are you running from one thing to another? How well would you do without your phone or smart-watch for an hour or even thirty minutes? Do you always need noise in the background and find it difficult to be in silence?

If you answer yes to one or more of these questions, chances are that you, like many others, have become trapped in a stress loop, causing some level of dopamine addiction. According to Susan Weinschenk, Ph.D.:

> Dopamine makes you addicted to seeking information in an
> endless loop … [It] causes you to want, desire, seek out, and
> search. It increases your general level of arousal and your goal-directed
> behavior. From an evolutionary standpoint this is critical. The
> dopamine seeking system keeps you motivated to move through
> your world, learn, and survive… [However] this constant stimulation
> of the dopamine system can be exhausting. And the constant
> switching of attention makes it hard to get anything accomplished.

"Prayer and meditation take you beyond the chatter of your mind and connect you to your inner compass."

For many people, including me, meditation is easier said than done. I used to beat myself up when I found it challenging to calm my mind and transition from being busy into slowing down and meditating. Nowadays, I acknowledge the restlessness I feel as I shift into a lower gear and remind myself that my body is simply adjusting to a different chemical balance (detoxing from dopamine). The higher my stress levels, the longer it usually takes to calm my mind and body and get into a deeper state of awareness. I have accepted that this is simply the way it is, and I have learned to be more patient.

Even though I have experienced many positive effects from meditation, at times I find myself coming up with some reason to justify not meditating. It can be frustrating, but after many years of practicing meditation I can tell you that I always feel better after I do so. I'm still no expert, but I have found different ways that work best for me. When I'm very restless I often listen to guided meditations, such as those by James Van Praagh, Jason Stephenson, and other teachers. Apps like Calm and Insight Timer have lots of wonderful resources.

There are many different ways to practice calming the mind and body and get into a deeper state of awareness. You can Google the different varieties, such as *Loving-kindness, Body-scan, Breath-awareness, Kundalini, Zen,* and Transcendental Meditation. Many yoga studios and spiritual centers offer meditation classes, which is a great way to learn if you're new to the practice. Be patient and get creative when it comes to meditation. Try different types of practices and see what helps you the most.

Even guided meditation doesn't always work for me, though. I'll find myself in the middle of a meditation without a clue as to what I've been listening to, as I've been pulled into the swirling vortex of my mind chatter. One morning my mind was racing with endless to-do-lists and worries about one thing or another. I knew I needed to calm down, but my guided meditation wasn't breaking my mental spell. I decided to take another approach. I asked for guidance from the spirit world. Often when I am seeking answers I turn to my maternal grandfather. He passed away when I was just three years old, but I have a few fond memories of him and I know that he cared about me. A medium once told me that he was with me as a spirit guide. I have felt his presence at different times in my life and value his wisdom and support.

That morning, I felt guided to a painting in the room where I was meditating. I thought it might hold a clue or sign that my grandfather was with me, but after examining the painting for a while I couldn't make any sense of why I had been guided to it. However, I became aware of having entered into a deep sense of calm, brought about by my focused analysis of the painting. I noticed the brushstrokes, the various colors it takes to create skin tones, the play of light and shadows, the marvel of depth perception created by the artist. Even though I didn't meditate in the true sense, gazing at the painting helped me release the grip of my thoughts and allowed me to find my center again.

Besides the calming effect you aim for in meditation, you can also send out prayers or requests for help during this time to Source, God, the Universe, Great Spirit, or whatever you prefer to call it. Releasing your problems to the Universe helps you let go of your worries. This is easier to do when you come from a calm place, such as during meditation, when you are not so imprisoned by your fears. Worries keep you caught in a holding pattern, focused on the problem. Praying for help and guidance assists in shifting towards a solution. Albert Einstein said, "We cannot solve our problems with the same thinking we used when we created them."

When I get stuck in life and I have clearly identified my problem, I pray for help with it and release it to the Universe, to God. Once I make my request for guidance, I feel a release of energy, and I know I will receive an answer, solution, or sense of acceptance in due time. In a later chapter I will explain how I receive signs that lead me to these answers.

Prayer and meditation take you beyond the chatter of your mind, beyond your ruminations and fears, and connect you to the true messages of your soul. These tools help you discover and tune into your inner compass. I love Paramahansa Yogananda's take on meditation: "Don't feel badly if you find yourself too restless to meditate deeply. Calmness will come in time, if you practice regularly. Just never accept the thought that meditation is not for you. Remember, calmness is your eternal, true nature."

Now that you know how to connect to a more authentic part of you beyond the chatter of your mind, you are ready for something truly exhilarating: discovering what you deeply desire.

PART TWO
FINDING YOUR CENTER
SUMMARY POINTS

- Centering practices can move you beyond your worries and calm you.

- Solitude is essential for connecting to your inner compass, your intuition.

- Solitude provides the space to reflect and allows for deeper thoughts.

- Solitude allows you to uncover what would bring you more joy, fulfillment and deeper meaning.

- It takes time for the nervous system to relax, as stress is highly addictive.

- Journaling helps you process emotions and aids in clarifying your thoughts.

- Prayer and meditation can take you beyond the chatter of your mind and connect you to true messages of your soul.

- You are not your thoughts. You are pure awareness, which is different.

- By becoming the witness to your thoughts, you become more aware of your own essence.

- You are far more than what your conditioned mind believes.

Discovering What You Want

"Freedom is not the absence of commitments, but the ability to choose — and commit myself to what is best for me."

— *Paulo Coelho, The Zahir*

WHY NOT?

Around the time I started allowing myself more solitude and began reading books and journaling again, I also decided to make a wish list. I had read that doing so can create big shifts in one's life. It's a simple exercise: you make a list of things you dream of doing or of having in your life, or that you used to enjoy as a kid, and you start acting on them, without judgement. You basically tell yourself, "Why not?" and start fulfilling your wish list. Vision boards work in a similar way. Online tools such as Pinterest are effective too.

Creating my *Why Not?* list was a big step for me. I quickly realized that the process is easier said than done, as it brought up all my fears and insecurities. For example, before I had kids I'd occasionally draw or paint, just for fun. I had a little bit of talent and I'd always wanted to challenge myself and get even better. After about a decade without painting or drawing, I feared I had lost whatever little talent I'd had years ago and that my paintings would be an embarrassment. This would confirm that I had no creative ability, and that I would probably fail at following through on other things too. This negative mindset made it difficult for me to start fulfilling my list. Eventually inspiration and curiosity won out and I started painting and drawing again.

Once I let go of my judgement about what my art looked like and focused more on succeeding with my to do list, meaning that I would push through my insecurities about my talent no matter what, I was able to enjoy the process and realize that my talent was still there.

Making a *Why Not?* list can be a very powerful tool for uncovering what you truly desire. This process is important because it helps you connect with your passion, that which inspires and interests you. When you act upon your list, you start following a path that holds more joy and inspiration and that will lead you closer to uncovering who you truly are. It helps us live a more purposeful life.

Writing your list also uncovers your judgements about your desires, judgements that may block you from fulfilling your list. This helps you be more honest with yourself and reveals fears and limiting beliefs that hold you back from pursuing what you truly want. You might notice you have quite a few reservations about the process, and about some of the things on your list. You must give yourself permission to keep your list private and just start writing, uncensored.

Journaling about your hesitations regarding your wishes can be very useful. Writing down the pros and cons about something you want to pursue can help you find out if it's something you truly want. Also, keeping track of your journey towards fulfilling your wishes is a wonderful way to monitor your progress.

Some examples of items on a Why Not? list could be:
- going for walks
- trying a new sport
- making art, such as painting, drawing, or writing
- traveling
- cooking, exploring new recipes
- learning how to play an instrument
- learning a language
- starting a business

"You must give yourself permission to acknowledge the things you want to do or create."

PERMISSION

I have talked to many women, especially moms, who find it challenging to set aside time for themselves because they feel guilty or selfish about doing so. I was like them not too long ago. But I have learned that when we do, the rewards can be great, not only for ourselves but for those around us too.

You must give yourself permission to acknowledge the things you want to do or create. I struggled with this at first, but realized it was necessary to implement the shift I hoped for. It can help to write down why you feel stuck in your life and what you would like to see changed. This way, when you feel like giving up on your *Why Not?* list you can remind yourself why you want a change and get back on track.

The *Artist's Way* helped me a lot with following through on my commitment to the items on my wish list. Author Julia Cameron suggests scheduling dates to devote time and energy to the things you most want to manifest. This way, they move from being dreams to becoming actualized. This approach helped me give myself permission to set aside special time to paint or draw for a couple of hours a week.

Another wish on my list was to get help with cleaning the house. I was finally ready to let go of needing to do everything myself. I held myself up to a high standard and expected to do it all myself, or I'd feel I had failed as a wife and a mother. Many of us know the pressure of trying to be a super-mom. We want to look attractive, keep a tidy and presentable house, and make

"Courage is required when you start acting upon your wishes."

our kids behave in public. On top of that we're supposed to bake cupcakes for the latest fundraiser. And, at the end of an exhausting day, our husbands might be expecting a little attention as well! Social media, with its snapshots of perfect lives, pressures us to live up to all of this. When we don't, we feel inadequate. Letting go of some of the expectations I had for myself was a huge relief. Having the house cleaned by a service freed up more time for fun and meaningful things, allowing me be more relaxed and enjoy life more.

I understand that not everyone can afford to pay for house cleaning, but maybe you can identify with the same need to do everything yourself in order to feel good enough. If that's the case, you might want to try to find ways to get some help in different ways that won't cost anything or much. Maybe you could ask a friend to pick up some groceries now and then, or have your kids or spouse take over a chore.

COURAGE

Paulo Coelho writes in *The Valkyries*, "The first great virtue of those who seek the spiritual path: courage." Courage is required when you start acting upon your wishes. When I made my list and picked something to follow through on, it was very unsettling at first. I had a long litany of excuses for why I should just give up: I didn't have the time or money, it was too selfish, it was stupid, etc.

One of the wishes on my list was going to the beach by myself. I remember going for the first time as I tried to follow through with my Why Not? list. I couldn't keep from judging myself.

This is going to take way too long! I have too much to do at home.

Followed by: *What am I doing here, anyway?*

I remember thinking, *I'm at the beach … now what? Here's the sand and there is the ocean, but I can't relax. I'm wasting my time! What am I supposed to get out of this?*

Something inside urged me to keep going, insisting that there was some shift on its way if I pressed on. Over time it grew easier to allow myself to be in those moments of discomfort and let go of any expectations of what I should feel. I trusted that a positive shift would unfold somehow. Acceptance seemed to release energies to flow more naturally, with less resistance. This created a sense of calm and peace in me and rather unexpectedly brought more flow and expansion to my entire life. It takes time for the nervous system to relax, as stress is highly addictive. You must give yourself time to get used to doing something for yourself, especially if this is a new process.

Making a change requires courage. You may come across all sorts of fears and worries of what might happen if you follow through, or what others might think, but if you call forth the courage to take small steps, the rewards of doing so might surprise you. Small changes are easier to execute and will increase your chances of succeeding. I recommend not sharing your wish list with anyone until you've had successes and positive outcomes from working with it. One negative comment can make you give up. Keeping it to yourself is like protecting a delicate seed that's just been planted. You want to make sure it has a chance to sprout.

DEALING WITH FEAR

When you are first getting used to being with yourself instead of in the constant motion of doing, you might feel unsettled. Your judgemental mind, your Censor, as Julia Cameron calls it, might tell you to give up because you have too many other things to take care of and you are wasting your time. Or, you might experience a burst of inspiration, followed by oppressive feelings of fear and resistance that keep you stuck in the illusion of safety. As your heart hints at a desire, your judgemental mind might want to shut it down and play it safe so nothing in your life will be disturbed.

But if you want to create a shift, particularly a major transformation, you have to discover what's behind your fears and how to manage them. The more you inquire about your fears, the easier it becomes to follow through with whatever you wish to pursue. When you get to know your fears and dare to courageously connect with them, you discover that your worries are allies in disguise, helping you grow into more wholeness.

After a couple of years of following my path of spiritual awakening, I had done a lot of journaling. I discovered that I loved the process of writing and became aware of how many books had similar messages wrapped in different stories. I felt inspired to collect the many insights I had gathered from the books I read, along with my own life experiences, into a book of my own.

This idea excited me tremendously, but after the initial surge of joy, my judgemental mind took over. It told me this idea wasn't realistic. Who in the world was I to think I could successfully do such a thing? My rational mind was victorious over my heart's desire, and I pushed the idea away. I didn't add it to my ongoing, ever-evolving *Why Not?* list.

Despite my strong resistance, the idea of writing a book kept popping into my awareness. Every time it did, a little jolt of joy came with it, followed by the voice of my judgemental mind pushing it away again. My ego voice won the battle for several months.

One morning as I was reading and reflecting, the idea of writing my own book resurfaced. This time, though, I was in a deeper state of awareness. In this state, I connected to a realm that is outside of the usual time-space reality. It's an awareness in which I was less hampered by my past or consumed by worries about the future. This state took me beyond time and allowed me to perceive the bigger picture of my life.

In that moment it was clear to me that I was supposed to write a book. As I processed this awareness, I was filled with gratitude for receiving this guidance and at the same time, filled with anxiety about this new adventure. I decided to manage my insecurities by quietly getting started without telling anyone. I simply allowed myself to enjoy the creativity of brainstorming about the book: what it would be about, which books I would source, which quotes I would use because they inspired me so much, which personal experiences I would write about because they'd had a profound impact on me. The more I allowed myself to enjoy the process, the more I got hooked on writing a book.

> ## "The amazing result was that the world around me seemed to have grown much more wonderful."

Looking back, I see the value that solitude and centering hold for me. They allow me to uncover and pursue wishes on my *Why Not?* list. They were necessary to create the shift in my life that I deeply longed for. This higher state of awareness was a portal into clarity and deep insights beyond my ego, beyond my fears of not being good enough. Connecting with my fears and seeking what lay behind them granted me the opportunity to expand my courage and self-knowledge, and led to a deeper integration and acceptance of who I truly am.

AWARENESS OF THOUGHT

Doing things on my wish list that excited or inspired me created space in my mind. I started looking at things differently and wondered, *Why not?* about many things throughout my day, not just about the things I wanted to do for myself. I became much more aware of the many subtle judgements I had acquired over my lifetime. Asking Why not? helped me become aware of them so I could let them go. It allowed me to be more open and accepting of other ways of doing and being.

Witnessing my thoughts, like I mentioned in the section on meditation, helped me recognize how often I indulged in negative thinking. I was able to catch these thoughts and reframe more of them into positive and open-minded beliefs, accepting my circumstances just as they were. The amazing result was that the world around me seemed to have grown much more wonderful. I was less irritated by people while grocery shopping, and more compassionate toward annoying drivers on the road. I also seemed to have more patience with

When you want to draw something
into your life, you must not
only imagine it visually, you must
also feel you deserve it."

my kids. I experienced firsthand what Dr. Wayne Dyer meant when he said, "If you change the way you look at things, the things you look at change."*

Starting your *Why Not?* list and acting upon it can help you shift from feeling that life is happening *to you,* that fate is controlling your life, towards a sense of *taking control* over your life. By consciously making things happen because they inspire you or bring you joy, you feel more empowered and better able to handle the things in life you cannot control. Filling your own well by doing positive things for yourself gives you a bigger reserve for handling the inevitable challenges life presents at times.

Making such a list and acting upon your wishes has the potential to create big, positive shifts. Chipping away at my *Why Not?* list helped me become more open minded and, ultimately, led me to a completely new and extraordinary perspective on motherhood and on life. This process helped me release old, dysfunctional mindsets and beliefs, making room for deeper, healing truths to enter my awareness.

VISUALIZATION

Now that you know about ways to connect to and identify your authentic desires through tools such as reflecting, journaling, creating your *Why Not?* list and meditating, you can shift to actualizing your wishes. Visualization is one way to help manifest what you want. There's more to visualization than merely creating a mental picture of what you desire, though. When you want to draw something into your life, you must not only imagine it visually; you must also feel you deserve it and believe that it's possible for you to obtain it. In other words, you have to connect to your desire emotionally and energetically. You have to allow yourself to be so excited about what you want that any negative, self-defeating thoughts won't have a chance of getting your attention and filling you with doubt.

Over time, with experience, this process gets easier. You learn to trust that what you want will manifest. This is where the *Universal Law of Attraction* comes into play. The Law of Attraction operates from the premise that everything is energy, including our thoughts, and that like attracts like. This means that when you send out high vibrations by choosing to focus on positive thoughts, you will draw more positive situations and people to you. As Deepak Chopra says in his book *Creating Health: How to Wake Up the Body's Intelligence*, "What you pay attention to grows. If your attention is attracted to negative situations and emotions, then they will grow in your awareness."

The Law of Attraction by Esther and Jerry Hicks is a great resource for learning more about this topic. In their book they use the term *imagination instead of visualization*.

They explain that "visualization is often only a memory of something that you have once observed. By *imagination*, we mean deliberately bringing desired components together in your mind to create a desired scenario." They expand on this definition by offering this example:

> That feeling of *I have a good idea!* is your point of
> launching your creation. In other words, you have been
> mulling your thoughts over in your mind until you have
> become specific enough that when you hit upon the
> perfect combination of thoughts, your *Inner* Being offered
> you emotion saying, *Yes, that is it! Now you have it!*

It's not just about visualizing or imagining. It's also about using your emotions to attract what you want by feeling excited about it, by desiring it deeply. I find that over time, this process gets easier. The path of uncovering who you truly are and what you want encourages you to not only open up your mind, but also your heart. You simply have to connect to your feelings if you want to find out what would truly fulfill you. In turn, this process allows you easier access to those emotions and helps you with visualization.

The ability to manifest what you truly want can be intimidating or downright frightening. *What if it works and I get what I want? How powerful am I really? Marianne Williamson talks about this fear in A Return to Love: Reflections on the Principles of "A Course in Miracles":*

> Our deepest fear is not that we are inadequate. Our deepest fear is
> that we are powerful beyond measure. It is our light, not our darkness
> that most frightens us. We ask ourselves, "Who am I to be brilliant,
> gorgeous, talented, fabulous?" Actually, who are you not to be?

Fear of success is just as real as fear of failure. To manage these fears, it helps to start with small goals, just like when you start fulfilling your Why Not? list with attainable goals. When you stick with the process of figuring out what you want and work towards receiving it, you transform your life. No matter how scary this is, the only way to make a change is to move beyond your fears.

Here are a few tips to help you visualize successfully:

- Know exactly what you want. Vague ideas are hard to visualize.
  Use your journal to get as specific and clear as possible. Writing
  your goals down can help you sort out your true longing.

- Be careful what you wish for. Think about why you have the desire
  in the first place. Imagine some of the possible consequences if
  your wish was actualized. Is it truly aligned with what you most
  desire? And always add the following onto every request: This, or
  something better. This way, you don't limit yourself.

- If part of you doesn't feel worthy of receiving what you want,
  ask why you think you don't deserve it. Journal about this in a
  candid, honest manner. This can be very frustrating, and even
  painful, but extremely valuable to discovering who you truly are
  and becoming aware of the many — often false — beliefs we hold.
  Visualizing what you desire is not going to be successful unless
  you believe you deserve it.

While it's crucial to be clear and definite about what you're asking for, leave the delivery method up to the Universe."

- Don't worry about how you will receive what you want, or even try to visualize the way your wish would manifest. While it's crucial to be clear and definite about what you're asking for, leave the delivery method up to the Universe.

- Connect to your desire emotionally: imagine you just received what you longed for and are basking in excitement and gratitude. Feel it viscerally with your whole body. Savor and absorb those feelings of joy, delight, and accomplishment.

- You don't need to visualize for very long at any one time. In my experience, what matters most is the strength of your focused intention while connecting to your wish emotionally, feeling the excitement of already having it. Spending hours visualizing won't make much difference, because most of us cannot hold an image or sustain feelings of gratitude for very long. More likely, the longer we visualize, the more opportunities our judgemental mind has to creep in with doubts. As soon as this happens, stop visualizing and come back to it later when you can connect to it with confidence. I believe it's better to briefly, yet intensely think about what you want and profoundly feel the gratitude you sense from receiving it. If you do this frequently, it should do the trick.

- It's ideal to meditate right before you visualize. A calm mind, free from emotional turmoil, is much more effective at holding a concentrated intention.

"When we start waking up to a more
authentic and integrated version of ourselves,
we realize that receiving help or guidance
is part of our journey to wholeness."

When I visualize, I focus for a few moments on what I want and then I let it go. I surrender it to the Universe and trust that it's on its way. Again, what's most important is the energy behind the intention. It's about creating a feeling of profound conviction that you will receive what you want.

Sometimes it seems that what you want takes forever to manifest and you lose faith. If you're not getting what you've been visualizing, keep in mind that divine timing could be at play.

Our ten-year-old minivan was a little beat up, but it didn't have too many miles on it yet. It had broken down once, leaving me stranded on the side of the road. We'd had it repaired and it seemed fine again. My husband's car, on the other hand, was reliable but it was twelve years old and had lots of miles on it. We were ready to replace his car and get an SUV that would fit our whole family and would be comfortable on long road trips; I would continue chauffeuring the kids around in our old minivan.

After hours of shopping online and spending all weekend at car dealers, we were frustrated about the lack of luggage space and legroom in various models. But late on Sunday, we finally found the perfect car. It had everything we wanted: eight seats, all leather, lots of legroom even in the third row, and the luggage space had the biggest capacity in its class. As I tried the various seats to get a feel for the spaciousness and comfort for each future passenger, my inner compass was telling me it was the car for us. As a matter of fact, it was already mine, *energetically* at least. I could feel it: this was my car. Jim liked the SUV as much as I did. It was late in the evening and the dealership was about to close, so we said we'd think about it and left.

The next day, when I called to see how much the dealership could drop the price, he told me it was already being sold to another customer. I was thunderstruck. What had happened? How had I misinterpreted my conviction that the car was mine? What was wrong with my intuition? Frustrated and disappointed, my husband and I decided to hold off on purchasing a new car. Our minivan would just have to do on the summer road trip we'd planned.

A week later, I smelled something suspicious when I pulled into my garage and got out of my van. Looking around for the source of the odor, I noticed a long trail of transmission fluid on my driveway and the street. It was ten days before our summer road trip and I knew this was a blessing in disguise. We needed to fix the van, sell it, and start looking for an SUV again.

My phone rang as my husband and I drove to another dealership to look at more SUVs. It was the dealer I'd spoken with a week ago, asking if we were still interested in the SUV I'd inquired about. The people who wanted to buy it had backed out of the deal.

"Well," I said calmly, "let's see how much you can drop the price."

As soon as I hung up, I couldn't contain my excitement. *I knew we'd get that car!* Indeed, we did, and for a good price too. My inner compass had been right after all. Divine timing needed us to wait a little bit longer with the purchase or we would have sold my husband's car, which we would have regretted. Sometimes we have to be patient and let divine timing take place.

Another time, my husband and I wanted to move from Orange County to San Diego. The economy had taken a big dive, taking home values down with it. We were worried about losing a lot of money when we sold our house. However, I had read Shakti Gawain's book *Creative Visualization* and decided to try her suggestions.

In the morning before our kids woke, I spent half an hour doing some yoga stretches and meditating. I told myself the story of what I wanted to manifest in the present tense. I visualized how excited we were about having sold our house for top dollar. Certainty coursed through my whole body. I was convinced we could pull it off. Why not? I thought. I did this visualization every morning for a few weeks and took random moments throughout the day to visualize our success. Our house sold for more than we'd bought it for, and still has the highest sale price in that community as of today.

Practicing gratitude supports you in imagining positive outcomes. Gratitude helps you become better at identifying the positive situations and circumstances in your life. This can aid you during visualization when you connect to the positive feelings you imagine you'd have once your wish has manifested.

Harvard Health Publishing states, "In positive psychology research, gratitude is strongly and consistently associated with greater happiness. Gratitude helps people feel more positive emotions, relish good experiences, improve their health, deal with adversity, and build strong relationships."

Practicing gratitude not only makes you more optimistic, it also makes the practice of visualization easier. If I truly want something, I always begin by visualizing it. It takes practice to deal with doubts, but stick with it. After some successes you'll feel more confident and the process will get easier. I highly encourage you to tap into your authentic self to sense what you might long for, because when you try to manifest something from a higher level of consciousness it is also aligned with the Divine, with Source. In my experience, when my desire comes from a higher state of awareness, I quickly feel the conviction that I will receive what I want because it is for my highest good, and therefore, ultimately, also beneficial for others. In these situations it's easy to connect to feelings of gratitude and joy for what I'd receive. It helps to realize that anything you receive will only give you temporary happiness. True joy and peace can only come from within. Still, it can be fun and very helpful to use the tool of visualization to manifest what you desire.

PART TWO
DISCOVERING
WHAT YOU WANT
SUMMARY POINTS

- ♦ Making a Why Not list can be a very powerful tool for uncovering what you truly want.

- ♦ You must give yourself permission to acknowledge the things you want to do or create.

- ♦ It takes courage to move beyond your doubts and fears and follow through on your Why Not list.

- ♦ Becoming aware of thought patterns is helpful in realizing the effect they have on you.

- ♦ Visualization can be a powerful tool to help you get what you want.

- ♦ Keeping track of your successes is helpful. It allows you to look back and see how far you've come, while motivating you to keep moving forward.

PART THREE
TAPPING INTO GUIDANCE

Guidance

*"The most beautiful thing we can experience is the mysterious.
It is the source of all true art and all science. He to whom this emotion
is a stranger, who can no longer pause to wonder and stand rapt
in awe, is as good as dead: his eyes are closed."*

— **Albert Einstein**, *My Credo*

ASKING FOR GUIDANCE

I t's not always easy to ask for help, especially for those of us who believe that we should do everything ourselves and that getting help might be a sign of weakness. When we start waking up to a more authentic and integrated version of ourselves, we realize that receiving help or guidance is part of our journey to wholeness. Receiving divine guidance can be an incredibly powerful and even life-changing experience. I am still in awe of the process of paying attention to signs that might hold a response to something I have asked for guidance around. The moment I receive an answer I am mystified about how I was led to it, while a deep sense of relief and gratitude washes over me. There is rarely a straightforward, rational path to receiving a solution. It unfolds like a river playfully flowing, running its own course.

There are four steps to receiving divine guidance:

1. Clearly define your problem or issue
2. Ask Source for guidance
3. Surrender your problem
4. Prepare to receive

> ## "You can find many moments throughout your day to 'throw your request out into the universe.'"

The first priority is to define your problem or issue clearly. If it helps you to write it out, do so. Clarity is key. James Redfield's words in *The Celestine Prophecy* about receiving this kind of guidance are insightful: "The problem in life isn't in receiving answers. The problem is in identifying your current questions. Once you get the questions right, the answers always come."

This has been true on my path of conscious awakening. Whenever I don't clearly define my questions, I remain absorbed in my problems, spinning in circles. I end up looking at the same issues from the same perspective. This mostly has to do with the habitual mindset I had for much of my life. I believed that things were just the way they were and that I didn't have much control over anything. I lived in a state of victimhood, perpetually focused on how bad things were. I believed that nothing could easily change or be solved. Now I am more aware when I am stuck and know full well there's always a solution or perspective that can help me. I make every effort to clearly define my dilemmas before I ask for divine guidance.

The second step is asking for guidance. It doesn't matter if you appeal to God, the Universe, Source, or Great Spirit. There is only one Intelligence behind All That Is. You can call it whatever you prefer. What's important in this step is that you connect to your request with as much emotional sincerity as possible.

I find that the more desperate I am, the quicker support arrives. This doesn't mean you should turn every request into a dramatic plea, but during the darkest moments in my life when I've needed support the most, I have experienced Source's quick response. I believe this is because when we are in a deeply focused state created by our strong desire for help and our conviction that we will receive it beyond any doubt, we allow the answers to flow more easily to us. The stronger your intention, the stronger its magnetic pull to the answer. Your doubts are no longer in the way.

You can pray during meditation, which is a nice opportunity to calm your mind and focus on your request for support. But you can also find many moments throughout your day to "throw your request out into the Universe," as I like to say. Some of these moments might be while commuting to work, folding laundry (one of my favorites), doing the dishes, cooking dinner, right before you fall asleep, or as soon as you wake up (another favorite moment of mine). This practice puts you in theta brainwave activity that allows you to connect more deeply with your inner compass. Creating moments of solitude, such as going for a walk alone, also connects you with your intuition.

The third step for receiving guidance is to let go of your worries and trust that an answer is on its way. I like to repeat the mantra "Let it go," while placing trust in Source to find ways to support me. For many of us this is a difficult step. What helps me is to remind myself that ruminating about my problems has never gotten me anywhere except in a miserable state. If I remain in a negative frame of mind, I will have more negative thoughts and emotions. This makes it more difficult for a positive perspective or solution to come through. This is how the *Law of Attraction* works.

Abraham talks about negative thoughts in *The Law of Attraction*:

> As you are focused upon a little (negative) thought, you will feel a little (unwanted) negative emotion. And if you are sensitive to the way you feel and want to feel better, you will change the thought. It is easy to change it when it is a small thought and a small emotion. It is much harder to change when it is a big thought and therefore a big emotion. The emotion will be proportionate, in intensity, to the amount of thought that you have amassed by the *Law of Attraction*. The longer you stay focused upon what you do not want, the greater and more powerful that thought will become. But if you are sensitive to your emotions and you withdraw your attention from the unwanted subject very quickly, you will begin to feel better, and you will stop the attraction of this unwanted thing.

"In order to receive signs of guidance
you must move into a more receptive mode
and tap into your intuition."

In *The Power of Now*, Eckhart Tolle talks about how the ego feeds on negative thinking, and that part of us does not want to let go of negative thinking. In order to do anything about it, "there must be a small degree of awareness from which you are able to witness whatever is happening and notice that you engage in a stream of negative thinking and are actually liking it and not wanting to get out."

He goes on to explain that negative thinking can even become part of your identity, like when you habitually look for something negative to complain about. Tolle suggests asking yourself if these thoughts are changing anything or if they simply drag you more deeply into the hole. It helps when you practice becoming aware of negative thoughts and become curious about them. That way, you can learn to shift your awareness away from them. This allows you to get back to a state of calm with fewer negative thoughts and more peace.

From experience, I know that it's far more effective to ask for guidance and trust that it will come. This helps me let go of my worries and focus on a positive outcome. I've also let go of the belief that for some problems, there are no answers. I've adopted the new belief that there is a solution for everything. Sometimes the solution lies in a new perspective, a new way of looking at the situation, that helps me accept things the way they are without the circumstances changing in any way.

In order to receive signs of guidance you must move into a more receptive mode and tap into your intuition. It helps if you have practiced listening to the inner compass that nudges you to go left instead of right, and sometimes encourages you to do the opposite of what you think you should do. When you first practice listening to your intuition, there will be hits and misses. Over time you'll learn to differentiate between what probably comes from your ego, i.e. from your fears, and what comes from Source. Guidance never comes from over-thinking. As soon as you engage too much with the logical and analytical mind, you block your intuitive flow coming from Source.

RECEIVING GUIDANCE

There are many ways to access divine guidance. When you first practice using your intuition it can be difficult to determine if you have received answers. The Universal Law of Attraction plays a role in receiving guidance. The more you trust that the Law of Attraction will work, that "like attracts like," the clearer the answers will be and the faster they will come. This means you shift away from problem mode, away from the negative thoughts and feelings around your problem — especially those thoughts about how it appears impossible to solve your situation — which attracts more of the same and keeps you spinning in negative emotions. You move into trust mode: you trust there is an answer and expect it will come. You imagine the positive feelings you'd experience once your problem is resolved. When you energetically become aligned with the positive emotions that a solution will bring, you attract the solution into your physical reality.

Guidance often shows up when I least expect it. A few years ago, I was going through a tough time. I was filled with worries about one of our children, and I wasn't sleeping well. I woke up many times during the night and often found it difficult to fall back to sleep. One of those nights I was wide awake, riddled with worry-filled thoughts. Sleep was not going to come any time soon, so I decided to go downstairs. Feeling depressed, I walked down the hallway toward the staircase. I asked for guidance and support to help me handle my challenges. As I walked downstairs, I noticed some bright stars shining through the narrow window above the staircase. They seemed much more radiant than usual. I walked out onto the deck to get a better view, welcoming any bit of distraction from my heavy thoughts. When I looked up, the Big Dipper was in the center of my view, luminous against the pitch-black sky. I noticed that it looked like a kite with its string hanging down. I knew

"Awareness doesn't come through elaborate thinking and analysis. Awareness is a deep knowing, the most convincing knowing we can ever experience."

what this kite meant: it was a symbol for playfulness, for lightheartedness, for being carefree again. The Big Dipper became a symbolic permission for me to lighten up and find my inner child again. It allowed me to let go of the heaviness and find joy. If I could find some lightness, it would be better for me and for my whole family.

As soon as I received the message I was flooded with elation and gratitude. To top this magical moment, the Universe sent a shooting star underneath my kite, as though it wanted to validate that I'd gotten the message correctly. All of this happened in about five seconds. Awareness doesn't come through elaborate thinking and analysis. Awareness is a deep knowing, the most convincing knowing we can ever experience.

Symbols are sometimes used to give us support, like my kite. The meanings of symbols are often very personal; a symbol might have different meanings to different people. Connect to the emotions you feel when you interpret a symbol and go with your gut feeling about what it means to you. If you feel uplifted, you are probably on the right track. Often, the first interpretation that comes to you is the right one. You'll get better at interpreting them with practice, and you will develop your own language of symbols.

Another powerful moment for me was when I received guidance about whether or not writing a book was truly connected to my life purpose. I had asked Source: *Show me if I am meant to write this book.*

I clearly remember the moment I received the guidance I had requested. It was one of those perfect days that makes me grateful to live in San Diego.

My son was in pre-school that morning, so I had a little time to myself. I walked around the house, checking to see if any rooms needed attention. As I went through a drawer looking for something, I discovered a transcript of a horoscope reading from my teenage years, right before I went to college. At the time I was curious about whether I'd ever get married and about my choice of study — developmental psychology.

I had completely forgotten about the horoscope. I recalled going to the man who'd prepared it for me all those years ago. He told me I would have children, but it wouldn't be easy; something to do with worries about having the baby too early or too late, the timing of the birth. He'd been right; I had preterm labor issues with all my pregnancies. Then he'd talked about how I would be writing books. I was shocked when I read this part. I had completely forgotten about it. At the time I couldn't relate to the prediction; I didn't even like to read books, let alone want to write one. I had dismissed the suggestion as inaccurate. But now I was stunned to discover it in my horoscope. I was amazed and grateful that I had been led to the answer to my question. This is how I receive guidance and how I live my life now, trusting that guidance will show up. I simply throw my request into the Universe and follow the signs.

Your intuition can help you in different ways. Many of us have sensed the presence of someone behind us before we see them. Or we know who is calling on the phone before we answer the call. Many of us have picked up on vibes, positive or negative. We all sense when a person is comfortable to be around or when someone is irritated or depressed, even when we can't explain how we know this.

Medium James Van Praagh explains:

> So if you think of it like radio stations, and all around us are frequencies and waves of energy, microwaves, radio waves, television waves … there's a certain frequency or wave that mediums can attune themselves to which is a higher frequency, and that's really the spiritual dimensions. That's what I can do as a medium, tuning into those higher dimensions, I'm able to tune into that and receive impressions — whether it's feelings of things, visions of things, words of things, memories if you will.

Many of us experience picking up information this way, but we tend to forget about it or dismiss it as coincidence. I have had many occasions in which I had a thought and someone else picked it up, like the time I finished reading a paragraph in a special edition of *Life* magazine about the movie *The Sound of Music*. I'd just read that the mother of the Von Trapp children had died from scarlet fever. Right at that moment, Jim asked me, "I've always wondered how the mother died. Does it say it anywhere?" If we pay close attention to these moments, we will discover that they happen more often than we realize.

Sometimes it can take a little while before I receive a response to my requests for guidance. I will often ask repeatedly for guidance on an issue until I receive the help I need. But sometimes when I'm feeling impatient and about to ask yet again for some wisdom, an awareness floods me that I've made plenty of requests already. It is time to let it go. I need to shift from sending mode to receiving mode. In my experience, that is sometimes the very moment when a sign is right there waiting for me to discover it. I become alert and intensely focused on anything that I'm drawn to, whether it's something that catches my eye or an awareness to check something out.

One morning I was folding laundry. I was working my way through piles of clothing and linens when I became aware of my negative state of mind. I realized how confused and frustrated I had been about the topic of *purpose*. What mystified me was that I always believed that once I found my purpose, life would be a lot easier. I figured once I knew why I was here on the planet, I could work on my purpose with ease, with lightness, with a clear sense of direction. Thinking that I'd found at least part of my purpose in writing, I had become frustrated that the writing process wasn't as easy as I had expected. For a couple of days, I had asked for clarity regarding this. Now, as I was folding laundry, my irritation resurfaced. I realized that I could let it go, because an answer would surely come my way. I knew to switch to receptive mode. Immediately a book across the room caught my eye. It was *The Pilgrimage* by Paulo Coelho. I was drawn to it, aware that the book might hold the answer to my question. I picked up the volume and intuitively knew to look toward the back. I opened it and quickly scanned a couple of pages until my eyes found the following passage:

If instead of asking "What am I doing here," people would simply resolve to do anything that sparks enthusiasm in their heart. The gateway to Paradise lies in working with enthusiasm; it lies in love that transforms and the choice that leads to God. It is that enthusiasm that connects us with the Holy Spirit, not hundreds and thousands of readings of the classical texts.

There it was: The key to living with purpose, the key to the question "What am I doing here?" was *enthusiasm*. I had to find joy and passion in writing again. My initial exuberance about writing a book had worn off when my rational mind with all its worries and judgements had taken over, turning the writing into an obligation instead of an exciting project. I had forgotten that this is how we connect with our inner compass, with our authentic self: through whatever fills us with excitement, passion, and joy. This is where creativity and inspiration come from. I felt a sense of relief and expansiveness that allowed me to experience great creative flow with my writing later that day.

DREAMS

Another way to receive guidance is through dreams. Dreams help you process your daily experiences as well as provide support and encouragement at times. Dreams often carry symbolic meaning. The challenge is to interpret them. You can find lots of information online and in books regarding dream interpretation.

Many symbols in dreams seem to have universal meanings and books and websites can help you discover the meaning behind them. For example, Patricia Garfield, dream researcher, psychologist, and author, talks about cars as a universal symbol. If you are driving a car in your dream, it often represents your life. Ask yourself questions like, *Was my car out of control, too fast, stalling, not going the way I wanted it to go, etc.* Replace the word car with *my life* and you will probably gain some insight into some aspect of your life. Even though many symbols are universal, your dreams are very personal. Only you can discern the best interpretation of them. The more you work with your dreams, the easier it becomes to interpret them.

Dr. Christopher Sowton discusses various ways to interpret dreams on his website, www.christophersowton.com, and in his book *Dreamworking*. He also shares tips to train yourself to remember your dreams better. I used to have lots of dreams when I was a teenager and kept a dream diary. I was fascinated by dreams and even tried to train myself to wake up while dreaming. This is called *lucid dreaming*: having full awareness that you are dreaming. I remember having had a couple of lucid dreams during that time. I knew exactly what I wanted to do while dreaming: I wanted the freedom and control to fly wherever I wanted to go. I recall flying among birds, looking down on villages, rivers, and mountains. Those were exhilarating dreams, leaving me in awe when I woke up.

Most dreams help you process situations you've experienced in recent days and don't seem to hold much significance. Some dreams, however, feel so important that you feel the need to quickly write them down. These dreams hold transformative power. They are often very clear, and the energy you feel as you awaken from them is quite different, often lifting you into an elevated state.

I've had several significant dreams in my life. One centered on my family. This dream happened around the time my husband and I decided we wanted a fourth child. As I mentioned earlier, after two miscarriages I was completely discouraged. Uncertain whether a fourth child was part of some divine plan, I asked for guidance. The most amazing dream released me from my agony of uncertainty. In the dream, I was at a convention. A Native American Chief sat in one of the rooms. He was a very wise, spiritual man who would give advice to anyone who wanted it. As I waited patiently for my turn, knowing I'd ask whether we were supposed to have another baby, I closed my eyes. When I opened them again there was a sign that read: "Of course you are meant to have another baby, but don't wait. You need to conceive NOW." You can imagine the joy and gratitude I felt when I awoke. Nine months later we had a healthy baby boy.

GUIDANCE FROM THE OTHER SIDE

I believe that there are ways to communicate with our loved ones who have crossed over. In my early adulthood, a medium once told me my maternal grandfather was with me and that I could always ask for his help. I never paid much attention to this, not knowing what to do with the information, until one morning when I was on my way to yoga. I was feeling frustrated with life again and was somehow reminded that my grandpa was supposed to be with me, like that medium had told me many years ago. I thought to myself, I had better get some proof to believe this, because I can use all the help I can get.

When I arrived at the yoga studio the room was very crowded. As I put down my mat I realized I was right next to Michelle, a woman I had gotten to know a little bit. After class she told me, "I had a dream about you. There was an older man in it."

Michelle explained how she had been developing her intuition. She told me about some details in the dream, details I confirmed with my mom later that morning, such as the type of clothes my grandfather wore and the tools he worked with. I concluded it was probably my grandpa who had appeared in Michelle's dream. She told me that the old man had given me butterflies. In amazement I recalled how I had just thought about my grandpa that morning on my way to yoga and how the day before an enormous butterfly had circled around me and my youngest daughter while we were playing volleyball on our driveway. It was early spring and there weren't a lot of butterflies around yet. I'd even pointed it out to my daughter since it was a strange looking butterfly that I had never seen before, and it kept circling around us.

I still wasn't fully convinced it was my grandpa and asked Spirit for stronger proof. A couple of hours later when I was running errands, I got out of my car in the parking lot and reminded myself I'd better pay attention to signs from my grandfather, switching from *sending mode to receiving mode.* As I walked through the parking lot a small voice of awareness in my mind urged, *What do you see? Look around. Pay attention.* All I could see were some banners belonging to the supermarket. I couldn't make any sign out of that. I kept feeling the urge to look more carefully, until I noticed a very old convertible in a handicapped parking spot right in front of me.

I read the handicap plaque: Expiration date June 30, 2019. I thought, That's my husband's birthday. Kind of funny, but not a sign. Then I stopped in my tracks. My heart skipped a beat and I gasped. I had forgotten that

> "When you open yourself up to guidance by surrendering your worries, support can come flooding in, often allowing the universe to synchronize events for you."

Jim h*as the same birthday as my grandpa. I couldn't believe I'd g*otten my grandfather's sign so quickly on the same day I'd requested it.

I received several more signs that day and the next. That evening when I got our mail, our neighbors' daughter walked up to the mailboxes to mail a card. Her birthday is also June 30. Another sign my grandpa is with me, I thought.

The next day I still had my grandfather on my mind. As I checked the copy room at our school for any requests from teachers for copy jobs, I found only one assignment: putting booklets together about caterpillars turning into butterflies. There he was again. From then on, I've asked him to show me he's with me whenever I need his support.

I'm still not sure how he's guiding me, but confirmation that he's by my side is very comforting, like the time when my husband and I weren't sure if we should take our family to the Grand Canyon and Zion National Park. Those were on our bucket list and we wanted to cross them off before our kids were grown. During the trip, Las Vegas would be our basecamp. The city was going through record-breaking temperatures of close to 120°F. It wasn't supposed to be as hot the week we planned on being there, but the temperature would still be in the triple digits. My husband worried that our old minivan might not hold up in those temperatures. He had a valid point: if we got a flat tire or had engine trouble on some stretch of freeway where there was no cell coverage to get roadside assistance, it might end up being a nightmare in the extreme heat. Was it worth it?

The week before our trip I took our kids to the pediatrician for their annual check-ups. Our doctor had some concerns about an irregular heartbeat in one of our daughters. She told us to have her refrain from strenuous exercise. I asked her about extreme temperatures and explained about our upcoming trip. The doctor advised me to hold off until my daughter was checked by a cardiologist.

This made me even more frustrated and worried about the trip and about my daughter's health. We only had three days to get some answers before we were scheduled to leave. All our travel plans seemed to be falling apart.

I was able to get a cardiology appointment the next day at a doctor's office one hour away. I didn't care about the long drive because with our upcoming trip, I simply couldn't wait until the next week to get an appointment at a nearer facility.

As I drove my daughter to the cardiologist, I was in a state of anguish and indecision. Then I realized I had an entire hour on a traffic-free freeway. It was a gorgeous day and the scenery was breathtaking, with hills and mountains moving past us, exposing us to ever-changing horizons. I will always appreciate that kind of scenery with its majestic expansion because it is in stark contrast to the flat landscape of Holland where I grew up. As I relaxed a little bit, I realized I hadn't asked for guidance yet. I asked my grandpa to be with me. I kept asking for his presence and signs to prove he was with me while I prayed for my daughter's health and a solution for our upcoming trip.

When we arrived at the doctor's office and found a parking spot, I became aware that I had better pay attention to signs. We got out of the car and walked towards the medical building. As we got closer, I saw a beautiful yellow butterfly drifting towards the entrance. As I mentioned earlier, my grandpa had given me butterflies as a gift in Michelle's dream, so, at times, a butterfly is a symbol or sign that my grandpa is with me. But since it was summertime and butterflies were everywhere, I didn't let it count. I told him, "You'd better give me some stronger signs than that!"

The nurse who checked us in made us feel comfortable right away with her warm smile and positive attitude. She asked me for the date of birth of the policy holder, which is my husband.

I said, "June 30, 1963."

She replied, "That's my birthday too! June 30!"

I knew my grandpa was with me. I relaxed, amazed at how quickly I had received a sign from him, and filled with gratitude for it.

As we waited in one of the examination rooms and the lovely nurse with the June 30 birthday helped my daughter prepare for the exam, something dawned on me: the smock she was wearing was decorated with Eiffel Towers and everything French. I smiled. We had reservations at the Paris Hotel in Las Vegas. I certainly felt the universe was aware of my worries, even though I still wasn't sure this meant we should go.

The nurse left and we waited for the doctor to come in and tell us the results. I realized I had been staring at two pictures on the wall across from me, both of which displayed butterflies. I couldn't believe I hadn't noticed them earlier. It was yet another sign that my grandpa was with me all the way.

Finally, the doctor came in and told us my daughter was fine. The mild irregularities were due to some medication she was taking. She'd had a normal EKG a year earlier, so he wasn't worried. He didn't place any restrictions on activities for her.

I drove home feeling grateful for the results and mystified about all the signs I had received. As I got on the freeway I still wasn't sure about our minivan holding up on the trip. Then I realized we could simply leave very early in the morning to avoid the hot temperatures and arrive by 9 a.m. Problem solved.

When you open yourself up to guidance by surrendering your worries, support can come flooding in, often allowing the universe to synchronize events for you. When you are stuck in problem mode, you are less likely to receive answers. You must get out of your own way so that guidance and solutions can come through.

Another experience with someone who has crossed to the other side involved my mother-in-law. Florence, or Flo as she preferred, was the most generous person I've ever met, always giving and never asking anything for herself. She was a great inspiration to those who knew her.

One day I was cleaning out my wallet and I came across a prayer card I'd forgotten about. I turned it over and saw it was from my mother-in-law's funeral service. I looked at the current date, and it turned out to be exactly five years to the day that she had passed away.

Normally our family visits her grave on the day of her passing, but logistics only made it possible to do this on the weekend. I couldn't be there that day because of a sick child and felt kind of sad about that, but the moment I found her card it felt like she was giving me a sign that she was with me. I was also reminded of something she'd once told me about her mother: she didn't necessarily feel the need to visit her mom's gravesite because she felt her mom's presence in her own kitchen and living room. Her prayer card is on a little table in our front room now. I see it every day. The prayer on the back is the prayer of St. Francis and has become one of my favorites. It speaks to me, especially the line, "It is in giving that we receive."

We can also be conduits for others, channeling messages from their loved ones, just like Michelle conveyed a message from my grandpa to me. My dear friend Pat and I spend some evenings together drinking tea. These gatherings allow me to leave my busy house filled with kids and enter her tranquil, beautiful sanctuary. Pat is a very gifted interior designer. When the many candles glow in her home, the tension of my busy day melts away.

Pat decided that she wanted to dedicate our next tea-time to her mother, who passed away many years ago. Pat fondly recalls her mother serving tea in beautiful tea sets. She had come across one of her mother's pieces recently. She decided to find the complete set and use it the next time we met.

When I arrived at her house, Pat asked me to wait for her downstairs while she took care of something. While I waited, I checked out her bookshelves. One entire wall of Pat's dining room is filled floor-to-ceiling with books. Immediately, I felt drawn to a particular section. I looked at a few titles and chose *Queen Victoria's Sketchbook*. How remarkable, I thought, a royal who was an artist. It seemed the perfect book for me; I wanted to get some inspiration to start making art again. When I opened the book I noticed a handwritten inscription. It read, "Love, Mom."

Pat returned and I showed her my discovery. We both felt it was a sign that her mother was present. Somehow, her mother had guided me to the book so that she could give her daughter a message of love. It was a magical moment. The book also carried a message for me: "Talents should never lie buried. You have to uncover them and use them."

GUIDANCE CARDS

One helpful way to practice heightening your intuition while receiving guidance at the same time is by using guidance cards such as Tarot, Angel Guidance Cards, Goddess Guidance Cards, etc. This is a fun and easy way to get quick insights and helpful perspectives regarding your problems. I have used Medicine Cards by Jamie Sams and David Carson for over 25 years. Countless times they've brought fresh insights to help solve my challenges. This set of cards consists of 52 animals and insects. Whenever I encounter an animal or insect in real life and it seems to be a sign guiding me rather than just a random encounter, I can look up the meaning of the animal or insect and receive a new perspective.

I've had friends pull a card while they focus on an issue they'd like to resolve or gain insight about. If they're not familiar with using these types of cards, I shuffle the deck for them, fan the cards out, and have them pick one. I tell them to pick quickly. When you start thinking about which card to pick, you get out of alignment with your intuition.

The most important part of using the cards is that you connect with the emotions related to your dilemma, such as sadness, anger, frustration, worry, etc. Feel those emotions as you think about your situation and then ask for help before you pull a card. I usually ask, "Show me how to look at this situation, or show me what to do."

One lovely afternoon I sat outside in my sunny courtyard and used my Goddess Guidance Oracle Cards by Doreen Virtue. I was deeply relaxed and decided it was a good time to pull a card and get insight into a situation in my life. My 10-year-old walked over and asked if she could pull a card. I told her she could, but that she should have a clear question and tune into her feelings about the situation. She shared her concern about something and we both took a moment to focus on it while I gently shuffled the cards. I fanned them out and she pulled a card that truly spoke to her. It made sense to me too. She wanted to pull another card for another dilemma. She told me what it was, and I pointed out to her that it was similar to the first one but that she could still pull another card. I shuffled the deck thoroughly and fanned them out again. I sensed she would draw the same card because the same guidance would apply to her second question too. Sure enough, to her astonishment, she pulled the same card.

"These cards are magical!" she exclaimed. I told her the cards are not magical, but her intuition is.

These types of cards can work in different ways. Usually the deck comes with an instruction booklet explaining how to use it, but you can also come up with your own methods. For example, when I use the Medicine Cards, I know the right card for me is the card that falls out while I shuffle. This system unfolded for me over time. It works best for me. Experiment with your cards and see what works best for you.

Be careful not to overdo it by pulling too many cards, because you can easily lose the connection with the deep desire for guidance and your rational mind might pollute the reading with its doubts and fears. Doreen Virtue cautions, "You can ask the same question again for additional information and validation. Most of the time, you'll pick the same cards whenever the same question is asked. However, the card reading will eventually become muddy and unclear if the same question is asked repeatedly."

TESTING OUR INTUITION

Sometimes I want to see if my inner compass is still accurate, especially after I have had a bit of a "dry spell," with no need to ask for guidance and thus no practice with tuning in deeply. That's when I get creative and come up with ways to test my intuition. Tuning into intuition has a lot to do with *awareness of thought*. Often, you may not be conscious of what you're thinking or sensing. As you become more aware of what is going on in your mind you might realize that you were thinking about someone right before they called or before you ran into them. When you become more aware of your thoughts and sensations you might also intuitively know what will happen, like that an event will get cancelled or changed. Sometimes I'll wake up in the morning looking forward to meeting a friend that day but sensing that she will cancel our meeting. And sure enough, she does.

Another fun way to test your intuition is through games. One day I was playing Clue with my kids and decided that I should try to discern the three cards in the envelope. At the start of the next round I determined I would intuitively know the three cards one of my kids had randomly (and blindly) selected and put in an envelope. To their astonishment I was right — and was no longer allowed to play the game.

Another time I practiced using my intuition by randomly opening a photo album. I recalled some memories of my mother-in-law and noticed the album on the kitchen island. I intuitively knew that if I opened it up at random, Flo's picture would be there. Sure enough, when I opened the album she was in two photos. The only page in the entire album with her photos was the one that I had opened to.

It helps to keep track of your intuitive successes by writing them down. Also write down the intuitive practices you come up with so you can use them again. This helps build your confidence with discerning what your intuition is telling you.

Many occurrences in life are mysterious. Opening yourself up to the idea that there is more happening than meets the eye can enrich your life and empower you tremendously. Asking for guidance has improved my life in countless ways. Over time, you can learn the difference between deeply knowing something, versus your mind simply guessing. There is a different feel to it, a different sense of awareness. When you allow yourself to place meaning in signs and experience the positive emotional effects this brings, you create a more meaningful and richer life.

PART THREE
GUIDANCE
SUMMARY POINTS

- Asking for help or guidance is not a sign of weakness, but part of your journey to wholeness.

- Receiving divine guidance can be incredibly powerful and even life-changing.

- Surrender your problem to the Universe, to God, and trust that an answer will come.

- Guidance often shows up unexpectedly.

- Be aware and alert for any signs that could hold the key to guidance.

- Signs of support are often symbolic. It's up to you to interpret the meaning of them.

- Dreams can be very helpful in guiding you.

- Guidance cards are a fast and an easy way to get clarity.

PART FOUR
AWAKENING INTO WHOLENESS

My Great Awakening

"One does not become enlightened by imagining figures of light, but by making the darkness conscious. The latter procedure, however, is disagreeable and therefore not popular."

— C.G. Jung, Alchemical Studies

As I began to create positive changes in my life, I started to question many beliefs that I'd regarded as the truth. They were my views about life, myself, and how I thought I should live. I realized that for significant shifts to take place, I had to change some of my beliefs and become more open-minded. Creating and pursuing my Why Not? list helped greatly with this process. It exposed the conflicts between my desires and the limiting beliefs I held about them, including that I couldn't have what I wanted. The ideas I had held for so long — some since childhood — were holding me back. The only way I could live the life of my dreams was to change my beliefs.

For example, I always believed I'd be a good mother if I focused mainly on my children. I believed that education, especially higher education, should be a priority as this would ensure greater financial security and happiness for my children later in life. I believed that motherhood was a tough job but that once my children were adults I'd feel pleased about how dedicated I'd been as a parent.

For a long time I thought it was selfish to take time for myself beyond my basic needs. I felt guilty whenever I journaled or went to a yoga class because

"I had to reframe my beliefs around taking time for myself. I had to view it as an investment in myself."

my husband was hard at work at his job and didn't have the luxury of free time. He never made me feel guilty, but it just didn't seem right. I felt guilty asking him to watch the kids when he was at home so I could spend time alone. I was okay with this if I had to run a quick errand, but nothing much beyond that. At times he encouraged me to take a break but it was usually when I was close to burning out, especially after a challenging day or week with the kids. That's when I'd allow myself to leave the house without the need to fulfill any to-do lists. I'd go shopping, aimlessly looking for something I might buy, trying to clear my head. Or I'd drive to the beach, making sure I wasn't gone too long. I didn't truly enjoy those moments because I felt guilty and was disappointed in myself for needing the break, for not living up to the expectation of endless energy and patience I had for myself as a mother.

I had to reframe my beliefs around taking time for myself. I had to view it as an investment in myself, so that I wouldn't be so drained all the time. I suspected that if I were less stressed I'd be a happier mom and wife. My whole family would benefit. Once I adopted this new perspective and allowed myself personal time without the guilt, I enjoyed going for walks, painting, and reading books on spirituality and psychology. I noticed these activities made me more peaceful, even joyful at times, and the effect often remained for a while.

My inspiration for new ideas also grew, expanding my interests. The more I allowed myself this freedom, the better I felt about myself. I also gained clarity about what I enjoyed and wanted, which felt liberating. All these changes helped me realize I was more than just a mother. I rediscovered parts of myself that I had forgotten about, like my fascination with the big questions around our existence, life purpose, and possible realities beyond this one. This shift in my beliefs about selfishness created a new balance in my life and made it easier to handle the challenges of being a stay-at-home mother.

Getting clear on what I truly wanted and releasing my limiting beliefs about it also helped me know what I didn't want. I started saying no to activities I didn't truly want to participate in, and allowing myself to pursue what I did want, even if it stirred up some fear that I might disappoint others.

I became convinced there was more to life than meets the eye. Especially when I experienced phenomena that I couldn't explain rationally, such as synchronicities, or moments when someone seemed to have read my mind, or I had read theirs. Like the time I was cooking dinner and realized I had forgotten to broil the chicken. I'll just heat up some hotdogs. It's been a while since we've had them, I thought. Just then my son asked me if we could have hotdogs for dinner.

Or the time when I wanted to call Jim to see when he'd be home for work as I noticed my son standing near me. At that moment I realized that it had been several weeks since our son had called his dad. I let the two talk for a bit, and afterwards Jim told me that right before the phone rang he was thinking that it had been awhile since he talked to our son over the phone and how he wanted to do so.

The dreams I had that seemed to hold guiding messages for me, and the synchronicities that the universe lined up for me as support during tough times, convinced me that there was more going on beyond what most of us experience in our daily lives.

This was about the time I started to feel isolated in my own family. I felt uncomfortable talking openly with my husband and children about my spiritual insights and experiences. My husband is open-minded but rational and likes science-based evidentiary facts. Whenever I told him about some of the synchronicities that happened in my life, he'd answer, "Interesting coincidence," and leave it at that, not knowing what to make of it. I didn't feel it was appropriate or useful to share my spiritual experiences with my kids, even though I wanted to talk about them. I only mentioned my experiences when my children brought up the topic themselves. I was careful not to try to convince them that what I believed was the absolute truth, but rather to encourage them to keep an open mind.

I'd never been the preachy type when it came to spirituality and had thought our kids would determine what they wanted to believe later in life. I'd provide them with a good education, take them to church, expose them to different sports and activities, and take them traveling. But as I deepened my own spiritual understanding, I wasn't satisfied with being "the spiritual one" in the family. I wanted to share the spiritual insights I had gained with my husband and my children but none of them seemed interested. I was frustrated that I couldn't share my spiritual beliefs with them. My wisdom fell on deaf ears, and I couldn't make them believe what I believed, so I kept it to myself. But over time this didn't feel right anymore. I yearned to connect with my family in a deeper way. There had to be a way to resolve my inner conflict. I prayed and meditated and asked repeatedly for guidance on how to bring a more conscious awareness of spirituality into our family life.

I was hoping Eckhart Tolle had written a book on raising children and spirituality. He hadn't tackled the topic, but at the end of one of his books I found the publisher's page that mentioned the name of a blog. I knew this was a sign that I had to follow. On the blog I discovered Dr. Shefali Tsabary's book *The Conscious Parent*. Dr. Tsabary integrated everything I believed about spirituality, along with Western psychology, in an East-meets-West philosophy. I ordered the book immediately.

I was reading a few pages early one weekday morning when I came across a passage that grabbed my attention. I sensed it held a key to greater understanding:

> Whether we unconsciously generate situations in which
> we feel the way we did when we were children, or we
> desperately struggle to avoid doing this, in some shape
> or form we inevitably experience the identical emotions
> we felt when we were young. This is because, unless we
> consciously integrate the unintegrated aspects of our

"I rediscovered parts of myself that I had forgotten about."

childhood, they never leave us but repeatedly reincarnate themselves in our present, then show up all over again in our children.

I was mesmerized by this passage. I wanted to keep reading but I had to get the kids ready for school. I decided I would come back to the passage after I dropped off the kids and ran errands. Once I returned home, Dr. Tsabary's words came to my mind again and I reflected more deeply on the emotions from my past that were still present in my life.

The common thread was insecurity, a sense of not being good enough. I often wondered why I was not yet a fully confident adult. I'd doubt myself in social situations. After a conversation I'd wonder if I'd said the right thing, or if I'd made anyone feel bad by a remark that might have been misinterpreted. I don't recall when I started feeling this way. I felt like this as long as I can remember and had always admired people who came across as self-assured. I had assumed that complete self-confidence would somehow magically happen during my late teens and young adulthood. I'll find out why I'm still insecure one day, I thought.

Then a shockwave of certainty shot through me. There was no need to wait for my circumstances to change or for me to gain more knowledge. *Right now* could be my moment of truth.

I knew how to get the answer. I could use a process that had previously helped me gain understanding as to why I feared or avoided certain situations. In this process I imagine a situation and become aware of how I would normally react. Then I find the opposite response. I imagine myself responding in this new way and focus on the emotions and thoughts that arise, as these give me deeper insight into the fears and beliefs that lie underneath. Once I become aware of my fears, I can let them go. This fills me with a great sense of relief and peace.

I couldn't wait any longer. Standing in the middle of my kitchen I decided to find out why I always felt insecure and uncertain, as if I was walking on eggshells. I imagined myself as a young girl and tried to think of something that would have made me feel uncomfortable. Immediately, I recalled a situation in which someone had asked me a question. Anxiety had flooded me as I tried to figure out what to answer. I feared I'd say the wrong thing, make a fool of myself, or come across as stupid. I'd tried to rescue myself by scanning for nonverbal clues on the person's face that might give away the expected answer.

Now I imagined myself responding in the opposite manner. Instead of stalling and trying to figure out what the other person wanted to hear, *I knew I must answer what I wanted to answer without worrying about the other person's reaction.*

Instantly, a profound understanding filled me. *I tried to please others in an effort to avoid feeling horrible after someone's negative reaction.* I finally saw that another person's response had nothing to do with me. The realization that I could simply answer whatever I wanted, *that I had every right to do so*, was something I'd never fully believed. I had always been a pleaser, trying to keep things peaceful. Conflicts always made me feel awful, like my whole being felt the dissonance in the air.

Through the inquiry process I discovered that all of my insecurities came from believing that other people were better, smarter, or more important than me; that I wasn't good enough. I couldn't believe it was so simple, and that the truth had been right there all along. Deep down, I knew that all my feelings of not being good enough were a lie. Many people, even the brightest and most successful, suffer from feelings of inadequacy. An incredible sense of relief washed over me when I realized *I was more than good enough.*

As this awareness took hold of me, I felt an energy flow starting above my head, pouring over me and through me. I was showered with great relief and joy, mixed with a visceral sense of the most profound, unconditional love and complete acceptance that I have ever experienced. This healing

"I had come home. Unconditional love is what I came from and what I was made of."

love radiated far beyond my body and made me realize I was much more than my physical form. I had read about the human energy field or aura before, and now it made sense. I became aware of my essence, my soul. *I had come home.* I knew that unconditional love is what I came from and what I would reunite with after this lifetime. I knew I was made from this love. I was free from the burden of worries and guilt. Free from all the "should-haves" and "could-haves" of my life. Free from worries about the future. I walked with a new lightness in my body and breathed more freely. I felt complete, perfect. The words *I'm whole!* rang in my mind. I had no need to change anything about my life. No need to prove myself. I basked in my wholeness with freedom, joy, and a deep sense of peace. *I was enough.*

I totally accepted myself for who I was and how I had lived my life. My flaws and shortcomings didn't matter. They were simply part of the human experience. I understood that as humans we are wired to evolve, and only through our imperfections can we do so. Our flaws are nothing to feel guilty about. They are tools to help us get closer to our own wholeness. That's why we're here — to learn and grow in our awareness of who we truly are: eternal beings of unconditional love. I deeply sensed evolution was the universal goal, as though everything in creation carries an innate urge to evolve.

There was no elaborate process that took place, no angels descended on me, no bright lights or voices appeared from some other realm, but it was deeply profound. I knew I was forgiven for everything that I had ever felt badly about. There was only joy because I had learned and grown, and that was all that mattered.

While I felt forgiven, I also forgave everyone I had ever held a grudge

> "We are human beings and we make mistakes, but that doesn't mean we damage the perfect state of our souls. We are merely trying to find our connection back to our authentic selves."

against. They were doing the best they could, figuring out how to live their best lives while carrying their histories and their flaws just like I had. I had been drawn into their dramas and become part of their stories as they had become part of mine. It was this simple. I understood there were many stories I had been caught in before, but now I didn't have to take anything personally. I realized the importance of becoming more aware of my life, of my soul, and of my purpose.

We are human beings and we make mistakes, but that doesn't mean we damage the perfect state of our souls. We are merely trying to find our connection back to our authentic selves. Along the way we have trials and tribulations; we succeed and fail. I realized it was my own harsh judgement of my failures that made them so painful. But in the state of wholeness, immersed in divine, unconditional love, I felt deeply understood, not blamed and judged.

I also realized that my sense of not being good enough was a false identity; it's not who I truly am. It was based on false ideas, wrong thinking, and misguided interpretations. The identity no longer belonged to me. I could take it off like a jacket, revealing who I really was underneath. The relief I felt was incredible. I had finally discovered my authentic self. This entire transformation of my being, along with the awareness of new insights, happened within just a few moments, right there in my kitchen.

The state of wholeness that I experienced lasted about five days. Remarkably, I felt complete acceptance of every circumstance and situation in my life. Every morning I jumped out of bed at 5 a.m., filled with excitement about my incredible state of being, ready to start my day. None of my thoughts brought even a trace of negative emotion, such as feelings of overwhelm or exhaustion. I remained centered in a state of deep peace and love. I didn't have any problems during those days. It was as though I was an open channel for solutions to come in as soon as a problem arrived. Joy filled my being. I lived purely in the moment, filled with wonder. I was awestruck that I had not known about this way of being before and dumbfounded that I had not recognized how much distress my flawed thinking had been causing me.

At this higher level of conscious awareness I wasn't frustrated by little problems such as squeezing an emergency orthodontia visit into an already busy schedule. Nor was I troubled by bigger worries about my children and their future, like my previous ruminations about how they would ever turn into independent and responsible adults one day. It was clear to me that my children have their own inner compass guiding them through life, just like mine was guiding me. I knew that evolution was at play and that I didn't have to understand it all. I only had to accept things the way they were, without frustration, fear, or worry. I realized that I was no longer imprisoned by my previous thoughts, analyses, and worries about how to instill certain qualities or characteristics in my children. Instead I was filled with deep trust that I didn't have to figure it all out. Doing my best as a mom was all I had to do. I basked in this peaceful trust, knowing that life unfolds mysteriously and that many things were beyond my control, including my children's future. I had no more fears about not being in control over some situations in my life. I simply knew my worries wouldn't make a difference anyway. This allowed me to peacefully enjoy each moment.

I had no judgements about people anymore. I had always tried not to judge people because they were probably doing the best they could, but during weaker moments I was pulled into a judgemental state. After my awakening I could see how everyone was on their unique path of growth, trying to live their best lives while carrying all kinds of stories about themselves and their experiences. None of us could really know the content of anyone else's personal journey. I knew that all were forgiven for any mistakes or wrongdoings, just like I had been.

I was aware of how my limiting beliefs had dictated the way I lived, and

> ## "In my heightened state of awareness, I realized that our flaws offer us opportunities to grow."

I recognized that other people were doing the same. They lived in their mental worlds filled with beliefs about who they thought they were and how they thought life was best lived. These ideas had created the lens through which they viewed all of their experiences and the world. I knew many felt broken and flawed. They were not living from their divine center, experiencing their own wholeness where peace and acceptance reside, but from mental worlds filled with conflict and turmoil.

But I could see their wholeness, their beautiful essence beyond their worried faces and the stress they carried in their bodies. This inner seeing is hard to describe. It's more like a deep awareness, an instant understanding, which changed the lens through which I could see others. All of us are already whole. We come into the world whole and remain that way, even when we forget as we identify with the mind.

For the first time in my life I understood what it meant to love unconditionally. I had always loved my husband and our children, but I had never experienced profound love for and complete acceptance of who they were, with all their imperfections and challenges. Shortcomings and character defects are part of the human experience. In my heightened state of awareness, I knew that our flaws offer us opportunities to grow. And besides, flaws are only flaws if we judge them as such. We are here for our personal growth, and to aid in the evolution of mankind. One is never separate from the other. Both influence one another.

The days following my awakening were glorious, but I faced a bit of a dilemma. How was I going to tell people about what I'd experienced? I told my husband, bit by bit. I'd had some similar experiences in the past, although not nearly as profound and long-ranging as this one, so he wasn't too shocked. I wasn't sure if I would ever be able to tell anyone else. The biggest problem was finding the right words to explain what it feels like to be immersed in unconditional love with a sense of grace and freedom. Over the next several months, I tried to find those words and write them down. I also spent a lot of time in introspection, seeking to understand what I had experienced. I came across many beliefs that I reevaluated and now see in a different light. In the next section I discuss these, along with the insights I gained during that time.

Waking up to False Beliefs

"Whenever you find yourself on the side of the
majority, it is time to reform."

— *Mark Twain*

Viewing my world through a new lens during my five days of bliss, I realized that much of what I had previously considered to be the truth had been based on flawed thinking. Now that my perception had changed, so had many of my beliefs. I held some of my beliefs because others whom I identified with did too. This is called *collective consciousness* (sometimes called *collective conscience or conscious*). Nicki Lisa Cole, Ph.D., explains that it is "a fundamental sociological concept that refers to the set of shared beliefs, ideas, attitudes, and knowledge that are common to a social group or society. The collective consciousness informs our sense of belonging and identity, and our behavior."

Often my beliefs sought to prove or validate something, like my self-worth. After my awakening I saw the flaws in my thinking and changed some of my beliefs, including the following:

FALSE BELIEFS ABOUT HAPPINESS

In his book *The Happiness Advantage*, Shawn Achor writes, "We should put happiness before success, but we think the other way around: we think we will be happy once success comes." In his research he has found that the opposite is true. Happy people tend to be more successful. Many of us think of happiness as something that will be achieved in the future, when we finally reach this or that goal, or when our circumstances change for the better. Just like I thought that having a big family would bring me happiness. Much of this has to do with how we define things or situations, such as *a successful career, or, a good life*. These definitions are filled with judgements, because if we believe one perspective is *good or better*, then an opposite perspective must be *bad or worse*.

Many of us try to measure up to beliefs held by our culture, our society, and our families of origin. For example, we might feel pressured to get married and have children because our parents and others expect us to, even if it is not the situation we truly desire. The fear of being judged negatively or of disappointing others if we don't fulfill this expectation can exert enough pressure on us to go along with it in the hopes this will please others and therefore possibly also us. We think that fulfilling these beliefs holds some promise of happiness or personal validation.

Trying to fulfill these kinds of beliefs can be exhausting. Keeping up with a demanding job simply to afford your dream house and car, making your life appear great on the outside while fearing that anything less would feel like failure, might be costing you your physical or mental health, or your relationships. Trying to be a super parent who does it all can drain you, along with the fear that you can't handle not living up to your own high standards or what you believe others expect from you. That's exactly what had happened to me when I tried to be Supermom. I was exhausted because I was constantly disappointed in myself, never able to fulfill my own, or society's, high expectations.

Achieving a goal can only temporarily fulfill you. It's like you're running in circles. Your victorious highs quickly fade, tempting you to find another goal that seems to hold another promise of happiness once you reach it. As long as you continue to measure success and what you deem *good* in terms of external measures, like how busy you are, how much money you make, or your kids' grades in school, you will never feel completely fulfilled. True fulfillment is beyond measure. It is an inner experience, a state of being.

"Only when you know who you truly are,
what you love, and are passionate about
without judgement, can you sense the path
that resonates strongest with you, that
allows you to express who you really are."

When you feel satisfied with your life you have less need to pursue empty goals. You will be happy with where you are in life *exactly as it is*. You will also have more to give to others, because you are not so drained by your endless yearning.

It's easy to fall into the trap of buying into false beliefs when many others around you hold the same beliefs, such as placing tremendous value in education as a measure of future success. Before my awakening I believed that my children had to do their very best in school so they could go to a good college and ultimately get a good job for financial security. I believed this was their ticket to happiness. My false belief was that financial security ensured a greater chance of being happy.

During my awakening, I clearly saw this was not true at all. I deeply understood that our children have their own purposes here on Earth. They are meant to find their own paths in life and let their own inner compasses be their guides, whether that includes going to college or some other path. I could clearly see that these choices have to do with personal growth, not with placing more value on higher education. Some individuals might gain great personal growth and find more meaning in life by *not* going to college and instead entering the workforce right out of high school.

My fear had created my expectations. I feared I'd be a failure as a parent if my kids didn't go to college and get good jobs. These fears were all illusions, connected to my feelings of not being good enough. Once I acknowledged these fears, I realized they were ungrounded and irrational.

Fear of not being good enough, or of being judged by others puts you into a competitive mode of trying to fulfill your goals. Only when you know who you truly are, what you love, and are passionate about without judgement, can you sense the path that resonates strongest with you, that allows you to express who you really are. Only when you uncover your authentic self will you know what you're supposed to do with inspiration and true fulfillment. This is how you can experience more meaning and happiness.

FALSE BELIEFS ABOUT IDENTITY

Much has been written about the false self, or ego. Eckhart Tolle talks about ego in *Practicing the Power of Now*:

> As you grow up, you form a mental image of who you are,
> based on your personal and cultural conditioning. We may
> call this phantom self the ego. It consists of mind activity
> and can only be kept going through constant thinking.
> The term ego means different things to different people,
> but when I use it here it means with the mind. The present
> moment holds the key to liberation. But you cannot find
> the present moment as long as you are your mind.

When I awoke to my false belief of not being good enough, I realized I could discard this identity. The mental image I'd had of myself was false and had been replaced by my authentic self. I recognized my experience in a paragraph from *Reinventing the Body, Resurrecting the Soul*, by Deepak Chopra:

> This entire sense of self is a ramshackle construct, but you
> depend upon it because you believe you must: otherwise you'd
> have no idea who you really are. A new sense of self can replace
> this construct, one stick at a time, as you experience your
> awareness, go inside, and meet yourself. The person you meet
> isn't a flimsy construct. Instead, you meet openness, silence, calm,
> stability, curiosity, love, and the impulse to grow and expand.

> It becomes easier to throw away bits and pieces of the old one.
> The process takes patience: you need to meet yourself every day.

Going through my *Why not?* phase helped me replace my old self "one stick at a time." I let go of my limiting beliefs about why I should not or could not pursue something and expanded my view of myself and my possibilities. The idea of writing a book seemed unrealistic at first as I was still stuck in false beliefs about myself. I didn't think I could do it. But as I kept succeeding at other things I pursued, I became more open to the idea that I could write a book, and finally began putting my thoughts onto the page. The journey of awakening challenges us to examine the beliefs we have about ourselves and encourages us to let go of ones that don't serve us. Then we are free to connect more deeply with our authentic self.

FALSE BELIEFS ABOUT PURPOSE

I used to believe that life would get much easier once I discovered my purpose. But even though I was convinced that writing this book was part of my life's purpose, I struggled with writing it. I often thought to myself, how am I ever going to finish this book? It was hard for me to make a lot of progress. In the previous "Guidance" section I described how I found an answer to this dilemma in Paulo Coelho's *The Pilgrimage*. He writes about finding activities that spark enthusiasm. Later, I found another perspective on purpose in Eckhart Tolle's book, *A New Earth*:

> To sum up: Enjoyment of what you are doing, combined
> with a goal or vision that you work toward, becomes
> enthusiasm. Even though you have a goal, what you are doing
> in the present moment needs to remain the focal point of your
> attention; otherwise, you will fall out of alignment with
> universal purpose. Make sure your vision or goal is not an
> inflated image of yourself and therefore a concealed form of
> ego, such as wanting to become a movie star, a famous writer,
> or a wealthy entrepreneur.… An enlarged image of yourself or
> a vision of yourself having this or that are all static goals and
> therefore don't empower you. Instead, make sure your goals
> are dynamic, that is to say, point toward an activity that you are

"Our mistakes are meant to help us evolve."

engaged in and through which you are connected to other human beings as well as to the whole. Instead of seeing yourself as a famous actor and writer and so on, see yourself inspiring countless people with your work and enriching their lives.

Tolle explains that we tend to think of purpose as something big that happens somewhere in the future. That was the mistake I made with my book. I was thinking of it as a mental concept and a future goal. Of course we all need goals, but Tolle made me realize that I should look at purpose differently: it's more about doing things purposefully, with intention, and being fully present in the moment. As soon as you start thinking about the end goal you lose the connection with your enthusiasm again; you're not in the moment anymore. Your mind with all its worries and judgements takes over and drains the creativity that was flowing through you just moments ago.

FALSE BELIEFS ABOUT PERFECTION

To pursue perfection is to pursue a futile illusion. The state of perfection is a static state of being. Life is dynamic, forever changing and evolving, just like the universe. Mistakes are inevitable in the process of growth. During my awakening I realized we were never meant to be perfect as in *flawless*, but *we are meant to become whole*. We become whole by integrating every aspect of ourselves into acceptance, without judgements. Everything that I used to view as negative within myself I now accepted simply as part of being human. I no longer denied the "negative" parts of me but saw them as assisting in my conscious evolution. This is how I understand forgiveness: our mistakes are meant to help us evolve. With my awakening my shadow side was integrated into *wholeness*. I felt complete. I rested in peaceful wholeness without any inner conflict. All was accepted within me. The light and the darkness within us are a contrast we can use to awaken ourselves into wholeness. Both are connected to unconditional love coupled with complete acceptance.

After my spiritual awakening I came across the book *Mindset*, by Carol S. Dweck. Through her research, she uncovered that there are two different types of mindsets: a *fixed mindset*, believing that your qualities are carved in stone; and a *growth mindset*, based on the belief that you can cultivate and change your basic qualities. The fixed mindset creates an urgency to prove yourself over and over again while people with a growth mindset believe that "everyone can change and grow through application and experience."

Life is much more fulfilling when you focus on growth and learning, and not merely on end goals and getting everything perfect. I realized this in my higher state of awareness when I sensed there is no beginning and no end, but rather a continuous evolution and expansion of conscious awareness. If you focus on end goals as though they hold some promise of lasting fulfillment, you will continue to be disillusioned. When you line yourself up with a growth mindset — achieving goals along the path of growth — you feel a deeper sense of flow and fulfillment.

In his book *The Happiness Advantage*, Shawn Achor defines happiness as "the joy we feel moving toward our potential." The word moving also implies a dynamic way of being and growth. A growth mindset gives you a far greater chance of happiness than a fixed mindset that pursues impossible perfection, leaving you disappointed much of the time. As I went through my spiritual journey, I gradually shifted from a fixed mindset to a growth mindset, expanding my positive beliefs about myself and my potential.

It can be unsettling to examine a belief that you have held for a long time. Many beliefs lend a sense of comfort, of belonging to others who hold the same beliefs. This is one way in which we connect to others and if we change our minds, we risk rejection. But becoming more open-minded about your beliefs allows you more options. As you let go of judgements and high expectations, you will witness the positive impact doing so has on your life and on those who love you.

Going through my *Why not?* phase helped me become more flexible

"Consciously awakening to your divine self, to a more purposeful way of living, starts with the process of questioning."

in my thinking. Instead of rigidly holding on to how I had always done things, I allowed myself to take a more flexible perspective in which more was possible — like releasing the idea that I had to do everything myself. Being open-minded is far more relaxing than constantly feeling the need to validate beliefs and continuously acting to fulfill those beliefs. Fulfilling my *Why Not?* list cleared limitations that were merely mental illusions, such as the illusion that I didn't have the time to pursue activities for myself.

As I became more open-minded, my heart opened up as well. I grew more comfortable with being vulnerable, and less afraid of being judged. This process made me more joyful as it filled my life with more positive situations and deeper, more authentic connections with others. Brené Brown states in her book *Rising Strong*, "We don't judge people when we feel good about ourselves." This has been my experience, too. As I created a more fulfilling life, I became less judgemental of myself and others.

Consciously awakening to your divine self, to a more purposeful way of living, starts with the process of questioning. This process can be quite unsettling, but you cannot create desired shifts in your life if you insist on keeping everything the same, including the way you think. Often it's a shift in your thinking, in your perspective, that allows for an opening in which change can take place.

During my *Why Not?* phase I became aware of some of my beliefs and started questioning these. This process not only helped me change my perspective, it also increased my curiosity about the deeper issues of purpose and existence. Later, this awakened curiosity helped me better understand what happened to me during my spiritual awakening and how to integrate it in the days and months that followed.

PART FOUR
WAKING UP TO FALSE BELIEFS
SUMMARY POINTS

- ♦ Living up to high expectations can be exhausting and not as fulfilling.

- ♦ Many beliefs about happiness only hold temporary fulfillment.

- ♦ True fulfillment is beyond measure and comes from within.

- ♦ Questioning and redefining your beliefs can be unsettling, but is necessary on the path of awakening.

- ♦ Reflecting on the limiting beliefs that you might have about yourself is part of self-awakening.

- ♦ Your inner compass guides you to what is fulfilling to you personally. The same goes for your children.

- ♦ Purposeful living has to do with enthusiasm, inspiration and joy.

- ♦ Perfection is an illusion and holds a false promise of fulfillment.

- ♦ Having a growth mindset gives you a greater chance of happiness, because you know that your mistakes will help you grow.

Integration as a Key to Wholeness

"Wholeness is not achieved by cutting off
a portion of one's being, but by integration of the contraries."

— Carl Jung

After my awakening, I was eager to understand my experience better and continued reading books on spirituality and psychology in the hopes of finding deeper insights. During that time, I stumbled upon a passage in Brené Brown's book *Rising Strong*:

> If integrate means "to make whole," then the opposite is to fracture, disown, disjoin, detach, unravel, or separate. I think many of us move through the world feeling this way. The irony is that we attempt to disown our difficult stories to appear more whole or more acceptable, but our wholeness —even our wholeheartedness —actually depends on the integration of all of our experiences, including the falls.

Reading this passage was a big *aha* moment for me because I finally understood why the words *I'm whole!* kept repeating in my head. I *felt* whole, but I didn't understand why yet. Now the reason was clear to me: in this higher state of consciousness, connected to Source, all aspects of me, which I had previously judged as good or bad, had been accepted without judgement and with complete acceptance into an *integrated whole*. I had no judgement in terms of right or wrong, good or bad, anymore. I viewed everything from

"My own judgements about my shortcomings and weaknesses kept me from wholeness."

a cohesive point of view: the "good" and "bad" in the world were contrasts to help us grow into greater wholeness and would ultimately help us realize that we are divine beings bigger than our limiting minds.

Now I could remain in complete peace, even while recalling past situations that I used to view in a negative light. I saw these events through the lens of growth and felt only joy because I finally understood that my previous judgements were based on flawed thinking. I understood that my "mistakes" were merely opportunities for growth; I had learned and grown, and that was all that mattered. Guilt was an unnecessary creation of the mind. I saw every challenge in my life, past and current, as invitations for growth and evolution towards higher awareness, towards a state of wholeness beyond the mind in which suffering ends and in which peace, joy, and love remain. I was grateful for my challenges because they encouraged me to look for answers and brought me divine peace and joy.

My flawed thinking in terms of good and bad had caused the separation from my own sense of wholeness, and my separation from something that was bigger than me: God, or Source. Source is void of duality; there is only love, peace, and joy. My mind had created duality, and as soon as I believed in this duality, my peace was disturbed. My own judgements about my shortcomings and weaknesses kept me from wholeness. Many of us tend to focus on our flaws. When you learn to release these judgements by accepting them as part of the imperfect human condition we are all experiencing, you become more whole.

Integrating your fears — your dark side — means shining a light on them instead of running away from them so they can dissolve. When you understand that most of your fears are ego-based and not needed you can uncover the flawed thinking behind them and integrate them as victories towards your wholeness. Once I understood that integration is key to wholeness, I tried to view everything I read or reflected on in terms of integration.

INTEGRATION OF INTELLIGENCE AND ABILITIES

Shawn Achor describes in *Before Happiness* how he sees the integration of different kinds of intelligence — *IQ* (mental intelligence), *emotional intelligence* (the ability to regulate your emotions), and *social intelligence* (the ability to understand and relate to other people) — as crucial for success in life. Achor mentions that for some time companies and researchers have been arguing over which intelligence is more important. He argues that we need to integrate them:

> To be truly successful, instead of thinking about intelligence in isolation, we need to focus on how to *combine all our intelligences....* Yes, all these intelligences matter, but what matters most is how your brain knits them together. Thus the question should not be, which intelligence is most important, but how we can learn to harness and amplify them.

When we get stuck by focusing on which method is more important in a competitive and disconnected way, we tend to miss the point. Integration is often the healing method that serves us best.

I came across the book *Reset Your Child's Brain* by Dr. Victoria Dunckley while trying to deepen my understanding about how the use of electronic devices affects our brains and our behavior, especially in children. Once again, I stumbled upon the importance of integration, in this case related to mental health/brain problems:

> When it comes to mental health, we tend to seek symptom relief without defining what we want to move *toward....* But while illness is about how things break down — both in

function and in description — health is about integration. No matter what the condition, the goal is to move toward making the brain more whole. We want it to function as more than the sum of its parts — whatever those parts may be. The more integrated the brain is, the more resilient and capable it becomes.

There it was again: it's not about how we can heal specific, isolated parts, but rather about healing the whole brain, in an integrated way, so that all parts work together.

Dunckley continues:

We all have an intuitive "knowing" of what it means to be whole. Our language reflects this: When we speak of someone's ego or psyche being integrated, we might describe him or her as "so together," "resilient," or "with it." But if an individual's ego is easily fragmented, we might say, "She falls apart so easily," or "He can't handle any stress. He just comes apart at the seams." When a child's mind is organized, it's easier for that child to complete routines like getting ready for school. We might refer to that child as "being on top of things," while a disorganized child "can't get themselves together."

Dunckley cautions against the over-stimulation of the brain through electronic screen-time, especially in children, which can create dysregulation (disintegration) of the brain and can increase or even mimic behavioral and psychological issues. Dunckley suggests an "electronic fast" to allow the brain to reset and become more whole again.

During the blissful days following my awakening, I stayed away from my computer and didn't watch TV. I only used my cellphone as needed. I wanted to remain in that wonderful state and had no need for entertainment from outside sources. I sensed these activities would disturb my peaceful state.

I now understand why I need a little time to become fully present again after I've been on the internet for a while: my brain needs to reset. I have seen this in my children too, after they have been on their electronics. At times, they seem harder to connect to and in a more negative state of mind, sometimes even throwing angry fits and acting irrational. I limit their use of electronics and raise awareness in them by pointing out how they feel after playing video games or spending time in front of screens.

INTEGRATION OF TIME

I'm fascinated by the concept of time but it's tough to understand and explain it because we are habituated to linear thinking. Understanding timelessness requires going beyond the mind. To many, this sounds contradictory because we have learned to understand concepts with our rational mind. However, you can only understand timelessness when you experience it through your awareness. The experience is beyond words, just like love is.

In my higher state of awareness, time was irrelevant. My past and my future didn't matter anymore. The past appeared to be just events that had gotten me to where I was in that moment. I no longer felt emotionally attached to the stories of my past. It seemed like such a waste of time to think about those. Only now mattered. I had awakened to my true self, free from the burden of being weighed down by negative thoughts and false beliefs, especially the limiting beliefs of who I thought I was. Basking in unconditional love, I felt incredible freedom to simply enjoy being fully in the moment. I didn't become lazy or irresponsible, but rather completed my tasks with much lightness and joy. It was wonderful to allow each moment to simply come and go as I went about my day.

I no longer worried about the future, either. It didn't seem necessary or helpful because being fully present, without my busy mind distracting me, was the only way I could remain in my blissful state. I wasn't worried about the future, only excited about the wonderful possibilities it held without being obsessed with those possibilities. It was as though the past and the future were integrated into the present moment. Only now was important, because only now was I alive, only *now* could I feel bliss.

I was amazed at how much time and energy I had wasted ruminating about the past and worrying about the future. I felt great relief that I no longer had to live that way. I could simply enjoy basking in the present moment without any worries. I felt wide awake and more present than I had ever felt before.

I finally understood Eckhart Tolle's words from *Practicing the Power of Now*:

> To the ego, the present moment hardly exists. Only the past
> and future are considered important. This total reversal of the
> truth accounts for the fact that in the ego mode the mind is
> so dysfunctional. It is always concerned with keeping the
> past alive, because without it — who are you? It constantly
> projects itself into the future to ensure its continued survival
> and to seek some kind of release or fulfillment there. It says:
> "One day, when this, that, or the other happens, I am going
> to be okay, happy, at peace."
>
> Even when the ego seems to be concerned with the
> present, it is not the present that it sees: It misperceives it
> completely because it looks at it through the eyes of the
> past. Or it reduces the present to a means to an end, an
> end that always lies in the mind-projected future.

The Dalai Lama talks about external things and internal experiences in
relation to time in his book *The Art of Living*:

> We cannot identify time as some sort of independent entity.
> Generally speaking, there are external matters and internal
> feelings or experiences. If we look at the external things, then
> generally there is the past, the present and the future. Yet if we
> look closely at "the present," such as the year, the month, the
> day, the hour, the minute, the second, we cannot find it. Just one
> second before the present is the past; and one second after is the
> future. There is no present. If there is no present, then it is
> difficult to talk about the past and the future, since both
> depend on the present. So, if we look at external matters, it
> would seem that the past is just in our memory and the future
> is just in our imagination, nothing more than a vision.
>
> But if we look at our internal experiences or states of
> consciousness, the past is no longer there and the future has
> not yet come: there is only the present.

"I had many fears of being judged for my spirituality, and I was worried people would think that I was crazy."

To me, this is an interesting and helpful way of looking at the concept of time and what it means to be fully present: detaching from the mind-space associated with the past and future.

INTEGRATION IN DAILY LIFE

When I sourced the universe for a way to peacefully integrate my spirituality in relating with my family, I received answers through my awakening experience. One of the answers was to love my family and myself unconditionally and to see our shortcomings and challenges as ways for personal growth. The spiritual way of connecting to my family had to do with complete acceptance and waking up to my false beliefs, with seeing reality through the lens of evolution and growth, void of judgement. It had to do with waking up to who I really was, releasing myself from the limitations of my mind.

Over time, my spiritual way of being seemed to integrate more and more into my daily world, into social circles beyond my family. Paulo Coelho describes this process beautifully in his book *The Warrior of the Light*:

> Sometimes the Warrior feels as if he were living two lives
> at once. In one of them he is obliged to do all the things he
> does not want to do and to fight for ideas in which he does not
> believe. But there is another life, and he discovers it in his
> dreams, in his reading, and in his encounters with people who
> share his ideas. The Warrior allows his two lives to draw near.
> "There is a bridge that links what I do with what I would like

to do," he thinks. Slowly, his dreams take over his everyday
life, and then he realizes that he is ready for the thing he
always wanted. Then all that is needed is a little daring,
and his two lives become one.

This "little daring" was the hard part for me. It took me a long time before I
found the courage to tell people that I was writing a book and to talk about my
spiritual awakening and the insights I had gained. I had many fears of being
judged for my spirituality, and I was worried people would think that I was
crazy. I was careful at first, choosing wisely who I trusted with my personal
stories. I knew people could crush my dream of writing a book while it was still
fragile in its early stages of development. As my confidence grew I was able to
share my story with a broader range of people, feeling more confident that I'd
write my book no matter what others might say. Processing and understanding
what had happened to me by finding the right words to describe what I had
experienced helped me *integrate* my experience within myself more deeply.
This in turn, helped me talk about it with others more confidently.

Once I became more comfortable sharing my story, I was amazed at the
support I received. People encouraged me to write my book. Some wanted to
hear more, and some seemed to find comfort in what I shared. This helped me
feel more comfortable in my own skin and more connected and integrated into
the world. My vulnerability allowed others to be vulnerable also. Sometimes
they shared their spiritual experiences with me. For some, it meant sharing a
story they had held inside of them for years, afraid people would judge them
for it. They seemed relieved that someone finally understood what they had
experienced. They recognized the same unconditional love and deep sense
of peace from their own awakening moments. For one person his experience
meant a great release, at least temporarily, from a state of anxiety and depression
that had been his norm for much of his life.

We are wired for social connections. We are meant to be integrated into
our communities in genuine, authentic ways. When we isolate ourselves we
create a greater sense of separation from others and most likely also from our
authentic self. This can be unhealthy for our bodies, minds, and souls. Brené
Brown talks about belonging in *Daring Greatly*: "Because true belonging only

"When we are conscious of our mortality, we lean into the courage to move beyond our fears and live with wild abandon."

happens when we present our authentic, imperfect selves to the world, our sense of belonging can never be greater than our level of self-acceptance." Working on self-acceptance by allowing yourself to discover and pursue what you truly want to create in your life can make it easier for you to connect to others in an authentic way.

The same goes for the connection in a marriage or intimate relationship. Initially, disclosing my experience and new insights to my husband Jim was difficult. I only shared bits and pieces in the beginning, just to see how he'd respond. I feared there was a chance of us growing apart if he couldn't relate to my spirituality. Even though I knew he loved me, I wasn't sure how he'd feel about it and about me writing a book on spirituality. I was afraid that the changes in me would affect our marriage. I knew I couldn't expect him to become more spiritual just because I was doing so.

Once I had grown tired of ruminating over my worries, I decided to talk to him. I remember the day well. We had planned a nice dinner out, just the two of us. The restaurant overlooked the beautiful Pacific Ocean and the La Jolla Cove. We had a table by the window and admired the breathtaking sunset, its tones of reds and orange lighting the sky on fire. It was the perfect setting for a romantic dinner.

I was on a mission though, and after my first drink, I found the courage to tell Jim my sincere worries. I couldn't look at him directly, but from the corner of my eye I saw a slight smile on his face. When I finished explaining my concerns, he gently shook his head in disbelief. He calmly explained how it was all going to work out just fine. He said that he might live in a more rational world and I in a more spiritual one, but that we still have a lot in common. I still have a rational side and he also has a spiritual side, and that much of the time we both doubt our own worlds anyway, so staying open-minded is the best way to look at things. He told me I could write whatever I wanted, and that he'd be there for me no matter what.

Filled with gratitude and a deeper sense of connection between us, I looked out at the perfect sunset. Having let go of my worries, I fully absorbed the gorgeous view. I also became aware of people around me. The whole restaurant came alive with all the guests admiring the view, enjoying their meals and their dining companions.

Suddenly my serenity was disturbed as I noticed a jet ski speeding frantically back and forth across the water. A moment later lifeguards rushed past in their speedboat, chasing the jet ski to the edge of the cove. An ambulance with flashing lights pulled up to the water, drawing a crowd of spectators. A medical helicopter hovered overhead. As guests in the restaurant alerted one another to the scene that was unfolding below our window, one victim was airlifted and another taken away in the ambulance. A story quickly took shape: two people had fallen off the cliff. One of them survived and one did not.

The profound contrast between our romantic evening and my personal mission — and the life and death situation — made me deeply aware of my own mortality. Life can be so full and amazing, and at the same time so fragile. All of this made me even more appreciative of my commitment to live more fully. When we are conscious of our mortality, we lean into the courage to move beyond our fears and live with wild abandon.

PART FOUR
INTEGRATION AS A KEY
TO WHOLENESS
SUMMARY POINTS

- ◆ When you integrate your shortcomings within yourself through acceptance, seeing them as a natural part of the human condition, you will feel more content with yourself.

- ◆ Shedding a light on your fears, by finding out what's behind them, helps you dissolve them, increasing your sense of calm and peace.

- ◆ You will feel more centered when you are more present in the moment.

- ◆ The more you can be your true self in all areas of your life, the more grounded and whole you will feel.

- ◆ The more you feel connected to others and integrated into your community, neighborhood and family, the more peaceful and whole you'll feel.

PART FIVE
LIVING A SPIRITUAL LIFE

My Life Now

*"Only the wise know just where predestination ends and free will
begins. Meanwhile, you must keep on doing your best, according to your
own clearest understanding. You must long for freedom as the drowning
man longs for air. Without sincere longing, you will never find God."*

— *Paramahansa Yogananda*

During my five days of bliss, I was convinced I'd remain in that
state for the rest of my life. After all, I had come home; I had
become one with my authentic self. It was my birthright to be
in a state of unconditional love, free of worries. All of us have
this birthright.

When familiar feelings of discomfort seeped in little by little, I knew I was
losing the connection. This was difficult for me. Over the next couple of
weeks, the whole spectrum of emotions, including the unpleasant ones such
as sadness, frustration, anger, fear, and guilt became part of my life again. No
matter how hard I tried, I wasn't successful at reconnecting with that higher
level of consciousness. I fell back into old patterns of not feeling good enough,
self-doubt, negative thinking, and judgements. Inner conflict became part of
my mental world again.

Although I struggled with the disappointment and sadness of fading bliss, I
took comfort in knowing that I would return to it fully again one day. The state
of unconditional love would always be waiting for me. The new insights I had

gained gave me a greater sense of freedom and inner peace. I was less worried in general and more comfortable with pursuing new possibilities for myself.

What also helped me a lot is having a deeper understanding of *attachment*. During my days of bliss, I was *in* the world, but not *of* the world. I was more of a witness. I didn't get emotionally attached to situations or outcomes. I wasn't removed or cold. Instead, I fully accepted what was, without trying to hold on to something or change it. If I wanted to create certain situations but I didn't succeed, I didn't resist. Life simply flowed through me and past me.

Now that I am no longer in that elevated state of consciousness, I have to remind myself regularly to detach from my need for my circumstances or outcomes to be a certain way. I can let things go a bit more easily and be okay with however things unfold.

In *The Five Levels of Attachment*, Don Miguel Ruiz Jr. explains how different levels of attachment affect us in our daily lives. He clarifies:

> Our point of view creates our reality. When we are stuck in
> our beliefs, our reality becomes rigid, stagnant, and oppressive.
> We become bound to our attachments because we have lost
> our ability to recognize that we have a choice to be free of them.

This insight helps me when I sense my own frustration, anger or sadness with my situation, and reminds me to check how much I have attached myself to needing something to be a certain way, other than how it is in the moment. Often I realize I can let go of my attachment a bit, sometimes even completely. This helps me with staying centered.

Besides being aware of my level of attachment, I also know that every challenge holds something that I can learn from, often breaking old patterns when I do so, bringing me closer to wholeness. This perspective helps me release my resistance and the irritation that I experience at times. As soon as I am aware of my negative emotions, I see what I can do with them: whether I need to learn to let go, accept, or rather pursue something instead of staying stuck in non-action, tied to false beliefs about not being good enough.

I also check for old patterns of thinking that still get activated from habit. If it's an old, ineffective pattern it's easier to let go of and find a more positive

"Evolution and waking up to our own wholeness are the goals, and it often ends up being a messy ride."

way of thinking, like when I feel overwhelmed by all the things that I have to do. My old belief was that I had to do everything myself, but now I become aware of this quickly, and ask myself who I can ask for help. It's nice to have four kids who can lend a hand with various chores!

Often, if I can't find a new insight, I switch to simply tapping into the sense of trust that I had during my days of bliss. This trust is not as deep as it was back then, but it certainly helps me let go of worries that are ineffective anyway.

When I experienced wholeness — feeling that I was *enough* — the need to prove my self-worth disappeared. I knew that my past expectations, especially regarding my children's futures, had to do with my need to prove that I had been a good parent. Now I know that this is not true, and that the greatest service I can do my children is to create my own fulfilling life, showing them that we are all responsible for making our own happiness. Uncovering my soul's longing and fulfilling my dreams allows my children more room to choose the direction of their lives.

This deep awareness also helps me understand the *illusion of perfection*: the perfect parent or child does not exist. Evolution and waking up to our own wholeness are the goals, and it often ends up being a messy ride. These days, I encourage my kids to sense what resonates strongest with their soul's longing and to explore that path. Whether this means they go to college or not, I will support them on their journeys toward finding meaning in their own unique ways and in developing the highest, most authentic expressions of who they are. Knowing that they have their own unique purposes and their own inner compasses guiding them allows me to let go of some of my worries about their futures. This

> "Parenting is hard. Our kids don't come with a manual. We have to figure things out as we go, and we never stop learning and growing in our role."

doesn't necessarily mean they have more freedom in their day-to-day lives, or that I have expanded my boundaries for them. Children and teenagers still need rules and limits, especially in today's digital and media age. I tune in to each child to see what his or her needs are, as they vary greatly. They all still need my love and guidance. And my guidance is not going to be perfect, but I do know that my intentions always come from a place of doing the best I can with what I've got in the moment. And I deeply know that is good enough.

Just because I had an awakening and experienced unconditional love for my family doesn't mean that I have become a perfectly patient and understanding parent, constantly radiating love. I have good days and bad days. Sometimes I lose my cool and then feel guilty about it. Some days reminding myself that I'm doing the best I can and that nobody is perfect doesn't do the trick. On these tough days, the best remedy for releasing guilt for my not-so-proud-mom moments is connecting with mom-friends who know exactly what I'm talking about. Parenting is hard. Our kids don't come with a manual. We have to figure things out as we go, and we never stop learning and growing in our role.

Now more than ever, I find it essential to connect with neighbors and friends in my community. Not only for my personal need for connection, but also because technology is advancing at an impossibly fast pace. Even though my kids share quite a bit of what's going on in their lives, I know they keep things from me, because all kids do. I need others to fill in some of the gaps on what they know about the latest things that our children might be involved in when it comes to the internet and social media or other activities.

Many times, I have been grateful to other parents for sharing information regarding this, and other times their gratitude came my way for the insights that I shared with them.

When it comes to my marriage, I feel very blessed that my husband and I have raised our children as a team while keeping our connection as a couple alive. Through my awakening, I understand the importance of deep connection and integration in others' lives. In society today, with all the pressures on our children in terms of academic performance and with technology invading our homes and threatening our social connectedness, I find it essential to stay connected to my husband and our children. It's easy to become strangers if we're not careful. Our phones, computers, and TVs can be major traps for disengaging from one another. We make it a priority to not let this happen and do what we can to know what is going on in each other's lives.

Looking back, my life has been enriched in many ways since I started my journey towards more fulfillment, including in the area of friendships. It takes becoming more comfortable with our own dark side in order to be able to handle and receive someone else's heavy challenges in life and to show true compassion. The better I get to know people, and the more people I get to know better, the more I realize that we all have a profound story to tell. There is great need for true connection, but for many this is hard. When we allow ourselves to be more vulnerable, release the need to look better than we really are, and move towards feeling good enough, we open the way for authentic relationships.

I made the right decision to create a shift in my life. My dissatisfaction with my life's circumstances, even though they looked ideal on the outside, had been a signal from my inner compass to move in a different direction, onto a path of deeper meaning and more purpose. As a result, I gained new and healing perspectives on life and on motherhood. I am excited about the many possibilities life still holds for me.

GETTING STUCK AGAIN

Once I accepted that I was back into full human mode, I realized I had become stuck again, stagnant. I had to continue to find ways to shift into new, positive directions. It takes effort to shift away from negative states. I'm not a person of great discipline when it comes to this, but I've gotten better at sensing negative emotions, and knowing how to release them. The periods of negativity have become shorter as I have more experience with using the different tools and am more motivated because I know how beneficial they are. Shifting into a more uplifted and peaceful state is easier to do since my awakening because I know I have the right and the ability to choose to feel peaceful, regardless of my circumstances.

Deep peace and joy are our natural state of being. Our minds disturb this peace. Whenever I feel agitated or upset, I check my toolbox for ways to center myself again. I use my intuition to sense what I crave the most. Sometimes it is a walk on the beach or a guided meditation. Other times it's connecting with a dear friend, journaling, reading an inspiring book, or anything else that I sense will do me good. Sometimes, it's just a reminder to let things go and to trust the unfolding of my life.

What amazes me is how hard my ego still fights the part of me that wants to be centered and fully awake. I still have moments when I judge myself about this, but now I remind myself that negative thoughts are addictive. They work like a strong magnet and we have to practice releasing their grip on us. It's simply the *Law of Attraction* at work: what we focus on grows. Once I commit to releasing my negative thoughts, I am surprised how quickly I can shift to a more peaceful state. Often, a thirty-minute guided meditation will leave me in a better frame of mind. When I can remain in a deeper state of mindfulness, aware of my emotional state and thoughts much of the time, my peace and joy sometimes remain for a few days.

One of the challenges we might come across when we first start using these tools, is confusion as to which tool to use in which situation. To solve this, it helps to increase our sense of awareness. Being aware of our bodies, emotions, and state of mind is helpful in so many ways. Increasing this type of awareness helps us with sensing what feels off: Is our mind racing? Are we worried? Is our body tense? By knowing/sensing what doesn't feel right, we also learn to sense what we need and which tool we can use to get it.

"Once I commit to releasing my negative thoughts, I am surprised how quickly I can shift to a more peaceful state."

For example, when my mind is racing with a long to-do list, and my body is tensing up because of it, I know I need to slow down even though it's tempting to just work faster to get it all done so that my body and mind can relax after I've checked off all the items on my list. I know from experience that when I'm in this state of overwhelm, I become ineffective without much flow in my day. I must calm my mind and body *before* I start my day. If I don't, there's a good chance I'll hit all the red lights on the road, will be put on hold forever on the phone, will have to circle around the parking lot a few times to find a parking spot, and all this would add to my sense of overwhelm and frustration.

I'll sense I need to calm myself and do the rational thing that many people do naturally: make a list of everything that needs to be done. This helps to get it out of my head onto the paper (similar to journaling) and releases the worry that I might forget to do one of the things on my mental to-do list. Just writing this list reduces the thoughts whirling around in my head so I'm clearer and calmer. Then I take things off the list that can wait another day and focus on the must-get-done-today items. I might take care of a couple of quick things so I feel I've accomplished something, but I also take a few minutes to pull myself even more out of "overwhelm mode." I'll take it one step further and sense the best and fastest way to calm myself deeper.

What I choose can be different each time. I might go outside and look at a tree swaying in the breeze while repeating the mantra, "Let go." I might meditate for a few minutes and do some breath work with short inhales and longer exhales to calm my nervous system. I might pull a medicine card from my animal deck to see what perspective I need to help balance myself again.

It's amazing how quickly I feel a positive effect that helps me think more clearly and have more flow in my day.

I encourage you to practice sensing what feels *off*, what you think you need, and how you can get it. The only way to find out if it works is to try it. I think you'll find that as you gain some more experience, any effort you make towards centering yourself has enough rewards to make it worth it.

Another challenge you might come across on your journey of awakening, just like me, is a lack of inspiration — feeling *blah*. Sometimes I experience a period of flow, when things come on my path that I have prayed for, followed by the sense that it all suddenly comes to a halt. Basically, after flying high, I lose my momentum and get stuck again. It's like nothing seems to move, at least not in ways that excite me. Frustration sets in and I can't wait for something to shift, for my second cup of coffee to kick in, or simply for something to happen to break the numbness. At this point, I know that not much is probably going to happen, and I better dig into my toolbox and deliberately try one or two of them to help me shift energetically.

The first thing I try is checking my perspective. Am I really stuck or is everything I've worked on and learned simply settling down, finding ways to integrate into my being just like sediments settling in a wild river? It helps to know that the slower, uneventful phases are simply part of the process of awakening. If we were always riding high, we would probably stop yearning to grow and to do the work required. We'd probably become unrelatable to others who are not experiencing these highs, and I believe that ultimately, our connection with others helps us heal individually and collectively.

During my five days of bliss, I understood that there is no *end goal* other than to become whole again. Wholeness means becoming fully aware that we are divine beings beyond our stories, beyond the effects of social conditioning, beyond our DNA and our family histories. The growing of our awareness is never done. Feeling flat, uninspired, and dull are contrasts to help us know what it is that we do and don't want. Contrasts help us see more clearly what we want to reduce in our lives and what we want to expand. Our negative emotions help us navigate our way towards new heights, towards our authentic selves. If we allow ourselves to see it that way, we can use this dissatisfaction as a catapult, an energizer to help us push through the dullness and create some flow again. We can view these phases of stagnation as an invitation to sense what we need and how to get it. Maybe it's the perfect time to have some fun with some of the tools and check the *Why Not?* list to pursue one of the items on it and just see what happens.

Trying a new tool can be challenging. It can trigger doubts about using it the right way and leave us wondering if it will ever work for us. Using a new strategy or application is like learning how to ride a bike. At first, we lose our balance and might think we'll never learn how to ride it with ease.

The same goes for trying a new tool. When I tried acting on my *Why Not?* list by going to the beach by myself, I was completely thrown off by my doubts and fears and couldn't settle into whatever the situation brought me. I felt I was doing something wrong and others who were successful at pursuing their goals were probably just better at many other things, too. Now I know that it's like learning to ride that bike: practicing a new tool, such as meditation, journaling, or visualization, allows us to find our own balance over time.

With repetition we find our own way of riding without overthinking it. The same goes for learning how to use a new tool. We find our own way of meditating, of centering ourselves, of asking for guidance, etc.

PART FIVE
MY LIFE NOW
SUMMARY POINTS

♦ The less attached you are to certain ideas and beliefs, the more at peace you will be.

♦ Every challenge holds gifts for you.

♦ Parenting is hard and you never stop growing in your role.

♦ The perfect parent or child does not exist. Perfection is an illusion.

♦ The goal is to wake up to your own wholeness.

♦ You are enough, even with all your flaws.

♦ You are responsible for your own happiness.

♦ Pursuing your own fulfilled life shows your children that they can do the same.

♦ Your children have their own unique purpose, just like you. They have to find their own path, just like you.

♦ Today's electronics can be a major trap for disengagement from one another.

♦ When you allow yourself to be more vulnerable, you open the way for authentic relationships.

♦ Being dissatisfied with your life is a signal from your inner compass to move in a different direction.

♦ Using the different tools gets easier with practice. Over time, you will find your own way of using them and what works best for you.

♦ Open-mindedness and flexible thinking allow you to stay at peace more easily because you are less attached to specific results.

Spirituality in Today's World

"The intuitive mind is a sacred gift and the rational mind is a faithful servant. We have created a society that honors the servant and has forgotten the gift."

— *Albert Einstein*

In early 2020, COVID-19 coronavirus spread all over the world like an invisible force, changing our lives forever. Life as we knew it came to an abrupt halt. While schools closed, stores and restaurants shut their doors, and mandates were put into place to work from our homes, we were filled with fears and left with many questions and few answers.

Before this pandemic, life had been challenging enough for many of us. Our hectic lifestyles had already encouraged some to intentionally reduce stress. Now, with so much uncertainty and so many changes and challenges in our lives, centering skills like I describe in this book are even more essential in today's world.

As tragic and difficult as this pandemic may still be for many, there is an upside to it, if we allow ourselves to see it. This Great Pause is an opportunity for all of us to reevaluate our lives. Once we can move beyond the fears of uncertainty, we can take the time to reflect on what it is that we want to change in our lives, especially once the treadmill of life starts back up again. Do we want to go back to the same busy schedule? Do we want to keep a more simplified calendar? Are we still convinced about certain beliefs,

"This great pause is an opportunity to decide if we want to live with more intention, meaning and deeper purpose."

such as what it means to be successful in life, how to be a good parent or spouse, or how to feel good about ourselves or our careers? Could we allow ourselves to be vulnerable and examine our beliefs in different areas of life? Could we allow ourselves to change our minds on something we had been firm on all of our lives?

Not only is this a great time to reevaluate aspects of our lives, it is also a great time to courageously ask deeper questions such as "what do I really want to do with my life?" This could be the time to shift into a direction towards answering a deep longing that we hadn't been able to meet with courage thus far. This could be the perfect time to decide to live life with more intention, with more meaning and deeper purpose, and go on a journey to uncover what that might look like.

If you are ready to dive deeper, to get curious about what you still want to get out of life before it passes you by, then have courage, be patient, and start.

Starting might seem impossible. It might seem difficult to integrate spiritual practices such as meditation and mindfulness into your daily life, especially with the current challenges of this pandemic along with the many distractions and high expectations in today's world. But once you get more comfortable with using the tools to center yourself and are aware of the benefits, you will find that integrating spiritual practices is essential. I cannot imagine my life without spirituality anymore. I find it necessary to center myself regularly and to increase my awareness of how today's busy and full world affects me.

Part of consciously awakening to who we truly are has to do with noticing how the world around us affects us. It helps to practice scanning our bodies to see if we hold any tension somewhere after or while we are on social media, the internet, or watching the news. We should ask ourselves regularly how we are feeling and what we are thinking, and then make connections to what might have caused a shift in our body or our mental world. Making this a regular practice helps create beneficial situations while limiting those that pull us away from our center.

A few years ago, I realized that watching the news is too upsetting for me. The horrific stories about people in distress, along with listening to the desperation in their voices and cries, put me on an emotional rollercoaster. Within seconds of watching, I felt my shoulders and neck tighten and a knot form in my stomach. I felt sad and helpless. It was as though I could feel people's pain, but there was nothing I could do about it. With this deeper awareness, I realized no one benefitted from me being pulled into this state so I decided to stop watching the news. I had been practicing meditation long enough to realize how incredibly beneficial it is to be in a state of calm and relaxation. In this state, everything is easier: I don't get overwhelmed as easily, my kids don't trigger me as much, I think more clearly, and there is more flow in my day. This significant list of positives made me decide I didn't want to be pulled out of a centered state by the news anymore.

However, I soon realized that I had swung the pendulum a little too far in one direction and I wasn't well-informed about what was going on in the world. Now I get the news online, in limited doses, without the emotional interviews. Often, simply reading the headlines and scanning the article gives me enough of an idea of what's going on without putting me on an emotional rollercoaster. I also make sure I adjust the timing of when I read the news, such as well after a meditation, not right before.

Although it can be a challenge to weave spirituality into today's busy schedule, it's actually very beneficial to do so because it's harder to stay grounded within ourselves these days. TV, the internet, and especially social media pull us into a realm that often doesn't align with our authentic selves. They can pull us into a state of feeling *not enough*, as though we don't have enough, are not smart enough, pretty enough, or successful enough, etc.

> "It's about how well we can integrate our
> deeper understanding of ourselves and the
> world we live in into our daily lives."

I highly recommend checking in with yourself regularly. How does your body feel? Do you feel tension anywhere? How are your emotions? Are you angry, sad, or frustrated? How are your thoughts? Are they scattered and racing, or are they calm and clear? When you develop greater awareness of your body, emotions, and mental world, you will get better at identifying which situations pull you out of your center (a state of relative calm and peace) and into negative emotions, physical tension, or negative thoughts.

With greater awareness, you have the power to limit being exposed to those situations, or at least manage them in a way that works better for you. When we do this, we can then use technology to our advantage to help us pursue all that we want without it luring us away from our center. For example, we can use technology as a tool to research and pursue the wishes on our *Why Not?* list. Wishes that come from a deeper level of internal consciousness, not from the internet trying to persuade us to make more purchases.

We don't need to spend hours practicing a new tool, such as meditation, in order to master it. Just like learning how to ride a bike well, a few minutes at a time will do the trick. I find that the frequent use of various tools for short periods of time is more effective than longer practice periods. Most of us simply don't have hours a day to meditate and pursue things on our *Why Not?* list, nor do many of us have the time or the money to take a sabbatical or go on a retreat. There are many simple ways that we can integrate spirituality into our daily lives. Like a few minutes of journaling or meditation, a few mindful moments of asking for guidance, or of centering ourselves through breathwork. We just have to get creative when it comes to weaving spirituality into our daily lives. Ultimately, it's not about how good we get at using a certain tool, how well we can meditate, or how close we get to enlightenment, it's about how well we can integrate our deeper understanding of ourselves and the world we live in into our daily lives.

Life is mysterious and we will never understand all the *hows* and *whys*. All we can do is to surrender to it, accept *what* is, and do the best we can with what we've got. And while we learn to manage our fears about an uncertain future, we can choose to take a closer look and reflect on what has shifted in our lives. Do we like this shift or not? What changes do we want to make? With some courage and persistence you can find your answers and through applying the tools in this book, you can create the changes you desire and put yourself on a path towards deeper fulfillment and more joy.

PART FIVE
SPIRITUALITY IN TODAY'S WORLD SUMMARY POINTS

- ◆ Crises can be opportunities to evaluate your life.

- ◆ Integrating spiritual practices and mindset tools is essential in today's busy world.

- ◆ Being aware of how today's world affects you is important so that you can optimize situations and stay centered.

- ◆ Just a few moments each day using your spiritual tools can create positive shifts.

- ◆ Much in life is beyond your control, so acceptance of "what is" helps you remain centered.

- ◆ Following your inner compass is not always easy, but in the long run it will reward you with increased peace and greater fulfillment in your life.

PART SIX
Conclusion

Our Inner Compass never fails to point to our True North: the direction that our soul wants us to journey towards. When we look the other way, when we ignore deep desires and keep pulling in a different direction, unhappiness and other negative emotions arise.

When I experienced deep unhappiness, even when I felt it wasn't justified, I knew I had to make a change. I sensed there was a deeper truth to life and that I had a purpose beyond my day-to-day existence. Early on in my journey, I learned that my fears were my greatest teachers. They held the keys to my awakening. Using various tools such as meditation, journaling, and asking for guidance, I was able to connect with my fears and dissolve them, allowing me greater freedom and clarity to pursue what I most deeply wanted. This put me on a path of greater fulfillment and meaning in my life.

Today's fast-paced lifestyle poses great risks of distraction from knowing what we truly want out of life, from connecting to our soul's longing and our life's purpose. TV and other media are constantly luring us into buying more, achieving more, or upgrading to bigger and better lives, leaving many of us feeling that we don't have enough or even that we aren't enough.

We are inundated by distractions from the outside world, disturbing the connection to our inner worlds. Learning to ignore these distractions while tuning into your inner compass regularly benefits you greatly. Relaxing your restless mind and body by using the various tools I describe such as centering techniques — like connecting with nature — helps you calm yourself. Increasing your awareness of the present moment makes you much more aware of your thoughts and emotional states of being. Your emotions tell you if you are connected to your inner compass or not, if you are centered and grounded or not. No matter your circumstances, you can always tune into your inner world and find a sense of calm and faith. The ability to do so allows you to handle your challenges more easily. It takes time and practice to learn how to connect to your inner compass and tune into this peaceful state, but it's well worth the effort. In addition to getting to a more peaceful and calm state, something original will start to emerge from within you, untainted by old conditioning and old beliefs that don't truly resonate with you. This is the awakening of your authentic self, beyond your rational and conditioned mind.

The path of self-actualization is not straightforward, but if you take a leap of faith and trust your inner compass, you'll discover that by diving into the fearful unknown you start seeing reality through a new lens. Old beliefs are stripped from their layers of fear, revealing new truths which transform your life with new possibilities. With an open mind you can also open your heart, expanding your capacity to give and receive. Life turns into a richer experience with deeper fulfillment, truer connections, and more joy. When you dare to follow the path of inspiration and curiosity, you align yourself with a new and exciting direction, and the universe will respond accordingly with synchronicities, signs of support, and answers to help you along your path.

Feeling more confident in the direction of your life, aligned with your soul's desires, you grow into greater wholeness. You'll feel more grounded and integrated in yourself and in the world. As you grow more whole, you'll realize that there is nothing to do to prove your worth; you must simply be who you are on your path of evolving into the most authentic expression of yourself. That *is enough*. No matter where you are on your journey, *you are always enough*.

To help you create more of what you want in your life, I've created *The Inner Compass Guide*. This is a short and easy-to-follow companion guide to *Inner Compass Mom* that consists of both questions and suggestions. The questions help you become aware of the areas in your life that you may wish to change. The suggestions are meant to help you practice the various tools that I describe in this book.

I'd love to know how these tools work for you. Feel free to reach out to me and let me know how you are doing on your journey, and be sure to follow me on social media for the latest news on our *Inner Compass Living* community.

Wishing you inner peace and true fulfillment.

– Danielle

To receive a copy of *The Inner Compass Guide*, go to my website: www.InnerCompassLiving.com and click on The Guide.

Find me on Facebook under Danielle Kloberdanz and please join my amazing moms group *Inner Compass Moms* for support and inspiration. I'm also on Instagram under the same names. Hope to see you there!

Acknowledgements

This book would not have been possible without the support of many individuals. I'd like to acknowledge several people for their encouragement and input to help make *Inner Compass Mom* a reality.

Bridget Boland - for bringing out the writer in me and connecting me with the true essence of my book. My deepest gratitude.

Leann Garms - for showing up at exactly the right time and the right place. Thank you for making this book a reality and for believing in its message.

Kaspar deLine - for your dedication and patience with me as we went through many ideas and designs. Your creative input was paramount to making this book a success. A sincere thank you for creating this beautifully designed book.

My dear friends and extended family - for your endless support of me on my writer's journey and beyond. A special note of heartfelt appreciation to my dear friends Celeste, Pat, Patty and Vidya for all the support and love you have given me over the years. And to my extended family and many of you out there in my neighborhood and beyond, as well as my on-line community. You know who you are and I truly appreciate your patience, encouragement and friendship.

My husband Jim - for your undying support and endless patience and belief in me. You are my rock, still.

My children - *Isabel, Madi, Elise and Cooper*. All of you are my greatest gifts. My love for you has no horizons.

Resources

The Happiness Advantage, Shawn Achor

Daring Greatly, Brené Brown

Rising Strong, Brené Brown

The Artist's Way, Julia Cameron

Creating Health: How to Wake Up the Body's Intelligence, Deepak Chopra

Reinventing the Body, Resurrecting the Soul, Deepak Chopra

The Alchemist, Paulo Coelho

Aleph, Paulo Coelho

The Pilgrimage, Paulo Coelho

The Valkyries, Paulo Coelho

The Warrior of the Light, Paulo Coelho

The Zahir, Paulo Coelho

Reset Your Child's Brain, Victoria Dunckley

Mindset, Carol S. Dweck.

Creative Dreaming, Patricia Garfield

The Law of Attraction, Esther and Jerry Hicks

The Art of Living, Dalai Lama

The Celestine Prophecy, James Redfield

The Five Levels of Attachment, Don Miguel Ruiz Jr.

Dreamworking, Christopher Sowton

The Power of Now, Eckhart Tolle

Practicing the Power of Now, Eckhart Tolle

A New Earth, Eckhart Tolle

The Conscious Parent, Shefali Tsabary

A Return to Love: Reflections on the Principles of "A Course in Miracles", Marianne Williamson

Sayings of Paramahansa Yogananda, Paramahansa Yogananda

Journey to Self-Realization, Paramahansa Yogananda